This book shows that the Johannine Epistles have a distinctive contribution to make both to the Johannine tradition and to the theology of the New Testament as a whole. Their importance within New Testament thought, complementary to the theology of the Fourth Gospel, is seen to be one of tensions-in-unity between, for example, confidence and imperative, individual and community, and faith and tradition. The author's timely survey shows that – when understood against their original settings – the Epistles have continuing relevance, and contain rich potential, for the theology of the church.

NEW TESTAMENT THEOLOGY

General Editor: Professor J. D. G. Dunn,
Department of Theology, University of Durham

The theology of the Johannine Epistles

This series provides a programmatic survey of the individual writings of the New Testament. It aims to remedy the deficiency of available published material, which has tended to concentrate on historical, textual, grammatical and literary issues at the expense of the theology, or to lose distinctive emphases of individual writings in systematised studies of 'The Theology of Paul' and the like. New Testament specialists here write at greater length than is usually possible in the introductions to commentaries or as part of other New Testament theologies, and explore the theological themes and issues of their chosen books without being tied to a commentary format, or to a thematic structure drawn from elsewhere. When complete, the series will cover all the New Testament writings, and will thus provide an attractive, and timely, range of texts around which courses can be developed.

THE THEOLOGY OF THE JOHANNINE EPISTLES

JUDITH M. LIEU

*Lecturer in Christian Origins and Early
Judaism, Department of Theology and
Religious Studies, King's College, London*

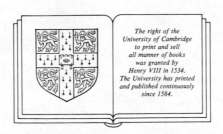

The right of the
University of Cambridge
to print and sell
all manner of books
was granted by
Henry VIII in 1534.
The University has printed
and published continuously
since 1584.

CAMBRIDGE UNIVERSITY PRESS

Cambridge
New York   Port Chester
Melbourne   Sydney

Published by the Press Syndicate of the University of Cambridge
The Pitt Building, Trumpington Street, Cambridge CB2 1RP
40 West 20th Street, New York, NY 10011, USA
10 Stamford Road, Oakleigh, Melbourne 3166, Australia

First published 1991

Printed in Great Britain at the University Press, Cambridge

British Library cataloguing in publication data

Lieu, Judith 1951–
The theology of the Johannine Epistles.
1. Bible. N. T. Epistles of John. Critical studies
1. Title 11. Series
227.9406

Library of Congress cataloguing in publication data

Lieu, Judith.
The theology of the Johannine Epistles/Judith M. Lieu.
p.   cm. – (New Testament theology)
Includes bibliographical references and indexes.
ISBN 0 521 35246 0. – ISBN 0 521 35806 x (pbk)
1. Bible. N. T. Epistles of John – Theology. 2. Bible. N. T.
Epistles of John – Criticism, interpretation, etc. 1. Title.
11. Series.
BS2805.5.L54   1991
227'.9406 – dc20   90–43045   CIP

ISBN 0 521 35246 0 hardback
ISBN 0 521 35806 x paperback

CE

Contents

Editor's preface

Although the New Testament is usually taught within Departments or Schools or Faculties of Theology/Divinity/Religion, theological study of the individual New Testament writings is often minimal or at best patchy. The reasons for this are not hard to discern.

For one thing, the traditional style of studying a New Testament document is by means of straight exegesis, often verse by verse. Theological concerns jostle with interesting historical, textual, grammatical and literary issues, often at the cost of the theological. Such exegesis is usually very time-consuming, so that only one or two key writings can be treated in any depth within a crowded three-year syllabus.

For another, there is a marked lack of suitable textbooks round which courses could be developed. Commentaries are likely to lose theological comment within a mass of other detail in the same way as exegetical lectures. The section on the theology of a document in the Introduction to a commentary is often very brief and may do little more than pick out elements within the writing under a sequence of headings drawn from systematic theology. Excursuses usually deal with only one or two selected topics. Likewise larger works on New Testament Theology usually treat Paul's letters as a whole and, having devoted the great bulk of their space to Jesus, Paul and John, can spare only a few pages for others.

In consequence, there is little incentive on the part of teacher or student to engage with a particular New Testament document, and students have to be content with a general overview, at best complemented by in-depth study of (parts of) two or three New Testament writings. A serious corollary to this is the degree to which students are thereby incapacitated in the task of integrating their New Testament study with the rest of their Theology or Religion courses, since often they are capable only of drawing on the general overview or on a sequence of particular verses treated atomistically. The growing importance of a literary-critical approach to individual documents simply highlights the present deficiencies even more. Having been given little experience in handling individual New Testament writings as such at a theological level, most students are very ill-prepared to develop a properly integrated literary and theological response to particular texts. Ordinands too need more help than they currently receive from textbooks, so that their preaching from particular passages may be better informed theologically.

There is need therefore for a series to bridge the gap between too brief an introduction and too full a commentary where theological discussion is lost among too many other concerns. It is our aim to provide such a series. That is, a series where New Testament specialists are able to write at greater length on the theology of individual writings than is usually possible in the introductions to commentaries or as part of New Testament Theologies, and to explore the theological themes and issues of these writings without being tied to a commentary format or to a thematic structure provided from elsewhere. The volumes seek both to describe each document's theology, and to engage theologically with it, noting also its canonical context and any specific influence it may have had on the history of Christian faith and life. They are directed at those who already have one or two years of full-time New Testament and theological study behind them.

James D. G. Dunn
University of Durham

Abbreviations

AB	Anchor Bible
AnBib	Analecta Biblica
BETL	Bibliotheca ephemeridum theologicarum lovaniensium
EBib	Etudes Bibliques
ETL	*Ephemerides theologicae lovanienses*
ExpTim	*Expository Times*
JBL	*Journal of Biblical Literature*
JR	*Journal of Religion*
JTS	*Journal of Theological Studies*
NCB	New Century Bible
NovT	*Novum Testamentum*
NTS	*New Testament Studies*
1QH	The Hymn Scroll from Qumran
1QS	The Community Rule (or Manual of Discipline) from Qumran (Both available in English translation in G. Vermes, *The Dead Sea Scrolls in English*, 2nd edn (Harmondsworth, 1987)
RB	*Revue Biblique*
SANT	Studien zum Alten und Neuen Testament
SBLDS	Society of Biblical Literature Dissertation Series
TDNT	G. Kittel and G. Friedrichs (eds.), *Theological Dictionary of the New Testament*
T. Levi etc.	*The Testament of Levi* (etc.) from the *Testaments of the Twelve Patriarchs*

TS	*Theological Studies*
TZ	*Theologische Zeitschrift*
WUNT	Wissenschaftliche Untersuchungen zum Neuen Testament
ZNW	*Zeitschrift für die neutestamentliche Wissenschaft*
ZTK	*Zeitschrift für Theologie und Kirche*

CHAPTER I

Introduction

The Johannine writings have long been recognised as contributing a vital element to the theology of the New Testament. Usually it is to the Gospel that we turn first in order to explore that contribution; the First Epistle is treated as a supplement while 2 and 3 John, on account of their brevity, receive little attention. Our task here is to allow the Epistles to speak for themselves; they have a distinctive voice to be heard both within Johannine theology and within the thought of the New Testament. To do that, and to avoid confusing their voice with that of the Gospel, we must first recognise their distinctive identity.

THE JOHANNINE LETTERS

As soon as we speak of a document as a letter we set up various expectations – we know what a letter is and the sort of information that will help us to understand it. We look for author (s) and for recipient (s), we expect it will probably reflect a particular historical setting and that it will convey information, exhortation, requests or similar material. A letter is not a soliloquy, the meditation or reflection of a solitary author, but a form of communication with others. Admittedly the letter form can be used as a device by an author who has no intention of sending it to the addressee, who may in any case be fictional; there are in the ancient world examples of letters of this type, where the form is an excuse to deal with a subject, philosophical or novelistic. It seems unlikely that any of the New Testament letters are of

this type,[1] although some may envisage a wider readership
than immediately implied by their address and nearly all are
considerably longer and more consciously structured than the
personal letters of the age.[2] Study of the Pauline letters had
taught us to be sensitive to these marks of conscious and
sometimes rhetorical structure, but still to root our exploration
of their thought in the circumstances and in the common
history of writer and of receiving church.

It is natural to seek to apply the same method to the three
'letters of John', but it may be neither possible nor right to do
so. The first in particular stands out as having none of the
obvious characteristics of a letter in a modern or an ancient
setting, and demands rather more discussion of what it is
before going on to the task of interpretation. The second and
third are more obviously 'letters', and with them we may
begin. The third, although least used in the history of interpretation and containing the least overt theology, would be most
immediately recognisable by its first readers as a letter. Its
length and structure parallel those of many other letters from
the early centuries of our era, and it includes a number of
conventional words and phrases – the words for 'please' (6),
the frequent address to the reader, the hope of a forthcoming
visit, and, most notably, the prayer for Gaius' good health (2);
the latter, despite its regularity in contemporary non-biblical
letters, is not otherwise found in the letters of the New
Testament or apostolic fathers.[3] It does have some distinctive
features – for example the absence of the standard greeting in
Greek letters (*chairein*: Jas. 1:1; Acts 15:23) or its distinctive
Pauline counterpart ('Grace to you and peace ...'); it lacks too
the usual Greek words of farewell, substituting the more
Semitic or 'biblical' 'Peace to you' (compare 1 Pet. 5:14). The
absence of a greeting may be an expression of the authority
claimed implicitly by the author, while the 'Peace to you'

---

[1] E. Hirsch, *Studien zum vierten Evangelium* (Tübingen, 1936), 177–8 suggested that both
   2 and 3 John were novelistic inventions, while R. Bultmann, *The Johannine Epistles*
   (Philadelphia, 1973), 1, describes the letter form of 2 John as fictional.
[2] See J. M. Lieu, *The Second and Third Epistles of John: History and Background* (Edinburgh, 1986), 37–8, 49.
[3] *Ibid.*, 43–4.

recalls the Johannine Jesus' words to his disciples after the resurrection (John 20:19, 21, 16).

The Second Epistle is a different sort of 'letter' and so must be interpreted differently. Although it too has a number of conventional phrases, it does not open with the conventional health wish of 3 John, but instead with an elaborate and overtly theological greeting in which the theme of 'truth' dominates (it is used four times in vv. 1–3). The greeting itself is of the type probably coined by Paul, 'Grace and peace', with the inclusion of 'mercy' as in the Pastoral Epistles; yet it is modified in a Johannine direction (Jesus is 'the Son of the Father'), and is turned from the implied wish of the Pauline formula to a confident declaration, 'there will be with us ...'. Another sign of a conscious appeal to Johannine language comes in the expressed purpose of the anticipated visit – a conventional theme also found in 3 John 14 – that 'our joy may be fulfilled' (v. 12: John 3:29; 15:11; 16:24; 17:13; 1 John 1:4).

While the recipient of 3 John is undoubtedly an individual by the name of Gaius, the 'elect lady' to whom 2 John is addressed is more elusive. The closing greeting from the children of her 'elect sister' (13) probably indicates that behind both women stand two churches with their members (the children). Although some have suggested that these may have been house-churches under the leadership of these women, the repeated 'elect' and the absence of names make it more probable that the women represent the church (es).[4] This rather artificial device, together with the lack of specificity in the letter as a whole, suggests that 2 John may have a wider audience in mind than one local church. The letter form, although similar to that of 3 John, is being used to make a more public statement, perhaps to those Christian groups which stood within the Johannine tradition. If this is so, the letter must be interpreted accordingly and not in the same specific terms as 3 John.

The First Epistle is a very different sort of writing. It bears none of the unambiguous marks which would characterise it as a letter, nor is there any comparable literature which would

---

[4] *Ibid.*, 65–7.

help us classify it. Neither writer nor recipients are named, and there is no reference to time or place and no greetings to third parties. Although not long by New Testament standards, 1 John is considerably longer than 2 or 3 John and than most contemporary letters. If the same author is responsible for all three – and this is not claimed explicitly – in 1 John he produced something very different from his other letters to an individual or church.

Yet like a letter, 1 John is written by an individual (2:1, 7, 12–14; see below, pp. 23–7) to a specific audience. It is apparently provoked in part by a particular situation (2:18) and so can hardly be an 'open' letter or a general encyclical. As shown by the repeated 'I have written', it sees itself as a written document and not as oral material which has happened to be written down (2:1, 7–8, 12–14, 21, 26; 5:13). It cannot therefore be classified as a 'homily' and it may suggest a physical distance between writer and readers. Other categories than a 'letter' have been tried, but most, like 'manifesto' or 'tract', are more an attempt to define the letter's purpose than a reflection on its form in the light of contemporary parallels. Even Hebrews, which starts abruptly without naming sender or recipients, closes with greetings and more specific references (Heb. 13:22–5). It seems that 1 John must be interpreted from itself using such hints as the letter offers, with all the problems of misreading that such an approach entails.

Thus, as with a letter, with which form it shares many characteristics,[5] the suggestions of specific situation must be investigated in order to put its thought in context. Yet its distinctive structure and style, which are not those of a letter, must also be accounted for. This 'distinctive' structure is in reality an absence of any clear structure, for the author keeps taking new directions or returning to old themes without constructing any obvious system. Proposed structures are almost as numerous as those who propose them, although the variety makes little fundamental difference to the interpreta-

[5] See F. O. Francis, 'The Form and Function of the Opening and Closing Paragraphs of James and 1 John', ZNW 61 (1970), 110–26.

tion of the letter's theology except where theories of source and redaction are involved (see below).

As regards style, it is the author's oscillation between two different styles that requires explanation and undoubtedly affects any interpretation of his thought. At times he encourages or exhorts his readers, building up an argument (2:1–2, 26–7), while at other times he uses abrupt antithetical statements which neither require proof nor brook disagreement, often in the form, 'he *or* everyone who …' or 'if we say …' (1:5–10; 3:4, 6–10). A number of scholars, following the initial work by E. v. Dobschütz at the beginning of this century,[6] have attributed these differences to different sources. If proven, this would allow the possibility of different theologies within the one letter. However, in the search to distinguish the sources, the presence of different characteristic theologies has proved almost impossible to establish;[7] hence in this study it will be assumed that any inconsistency of thought is to be attributed to the author and not to the use of incompatible sources.

Another approach to the antithetical passages has been to see within them a polemic against the opponents of the community who have recently left it (2:19; see below); the claims or actions which are categorically denied are the slogans or behaviour of the opponents, to be matched by the author's equally categorical slogans. Thus the antitheses and their theology must be interpreted within a polemical context, and the author's thought understood in terms both of what he is attacking and the fact that he is attacking. A number of modern commentaries follow this line, notably that by R. Brown.[8] We shall explore this approach further in the next section when discussing the historical setting of the letters. Yet clearly it is not a total solution; the author can use the antithetical style when there is no obvious suggestion of a debate with alternative views (as at 5:12), while in 3:4–10 the

---

[6] E. v. Dobschütz, 'Johanneische Studien I', *ZNW* 8 (1907), 1–8.
[7] This is recognised by H. Braun, 'Literar-Analyse und theologische Schichtung im ersten Johannesbrief', *ZTK* 48 (1951), 262–92, 264–70, although he still accepts the presence of a source.
[8] R. Brown, *The Epistles of John*, AB 30 (New York, 1982).

antitheses seem to be his own assessment of the case, not the contrasting views of two groups. In fact, the antitheses often arise out of the non-antithetical material which precedes them: the antitheses of 2:4–5 explain what is meant by the statement that the test of knowledge of God is keeping his commandments (2:3), while the antitheses of 2:9–11 arise out of the affirmation in 2:8 that the light is already shining. Moreover, the 'polemical' approach alone cannot explain the particular mix of types of material and structure of 1 John.

A further answer, therefore, has been to see 1 John as in some way related to the Gospel of John, explaining or supporting it, or even reclaiming it in the face of opponents who equally claimed to represent its theology. In support of this it is argued that the structure of 1 John follows the structure of the Gospel, both having a prologue, an appendix, and, less confidently, parallel internal divisions.[9] This would be highly significant for interpreting the letter, for one issue to which we shall return is how far 1 John should be understood in the light of the Gospel. This, as we shall see (below, pp. 15–20), can be done in more than one way, but even when 1 John is attributed to a later author who has not understood all the complexities of his mentor, its theology will appear differently when viewed within the acknowledged framework of the Gospel than when taken in isolation from it.

Undoubtedly there are parallels of thought and language between the two writings; a good example is the prologue of each writing (1 John 1:1–4; John 1:1–18), where both their position and their language evoke each other. An alternative explanation has been that the Epistle is a 'trial run' for the more developed ideas of the Gospel rather than modelled on it – so, for example, Grayston's commentary.[10] Both explanations have their strengths and weaknesses, and may depend

[9] Ibid., 90–2, 123–9; A. Feuillet 'Etude structurale de la première épitre de saint Jean', in Neues Testament und Geschichte, ed. H. Baltensweiler and B. Reicke (Tübingen, 1972), 307–27, argues that their parallel structure reflects the structure of the Christian life. As we shall see, elsewhere Feuillet sees an essential theological unity between the two writings (see ch. 2, nn. 31,81 below).

[10] K. Grayston, The Johannine Epistles, NCB (Grand Rapids and Basingstoke, 1984), 12–14.

on which sort of development seems more congenial, from simple draft to sophisticated art, or from complex whole to more mundane copy. A middle path has been to interpret the Epistle as a 'companion piece' to the Gospel, perhaps introducing it and easing its way. This too assumes a degree of cross-reference between the two, but also a degree of complementarity.[11] Certainly, 1 John cannot be interpreted without a prior decision as to whether or not the Gospel is to be presupposed. The approach adopted in this study assumes that the structural conformity between Gospel and Epistle is not at all evident, and that the relationship of thought can only be explored after first studying 1 John. In fact we shall see that the considerable differences in emphasis between the two writings mean that knowledge of one by the other cannot be taken for granted. As far as possible 1 John will be interpreted in its own terms, and the task of setting it into a wider Johannine framework left until a later stage (ch. 3).

A rather different approach to the peculiar structure and style of 1 John has been to interpret it as a reworking or editing of an earlier tradition or source which was itself by the same author or with which he was in fundamental agreement.[12] This is a development of the source theories earlier mentioned, but allows for an overall theological unity in the letter and concentrates our attention on the author's commentary on or modification of his underlying source. On the whole such theories have not won a large following, for they are difficult to prove and the procedure is a difficult one to envisage. However, the most detailed of those, that by W. Nauck, does direct our attention to a further important question: if the author is using earlier traditions in some form, what was their original setting? Nauck noted that much of the language and imagery of 1 John may in other contexts be associated with baptism; thus although baptism is not explicitly mentioned, the author may

---

[11] So, for example, J. B. Lightfoot, *Biblical Essays* (London, 1893), 194–8. While 1 John may have fulfilled the function of 'easing the way' for the Gospel in its early history, it is difficult to prove that this was its original purpose, which does seem more specific.

[12] So W. Nauck, *Die Tradition und der Charakter des ersten Johannesbriefes*, WUNT 3 (Tübingen, 1957); J. C. O'Neill, *The Puzzle of 1 John* (London, 1966).

be recalling his audience to their baptismal certainties in the face of the departure of the schismatics. This would affect our understanding of the language of assurance such as 'you have conquered the evil one' (2:14); this could be affirmed in the baptismal setting with its context of confession, commitment and claiming the victory won by Christ, without carrying the full weight of perfectionism implied when it is read as a generalised statement. Again this is a case where our decision about the nature of 1 John affects our understanding of its thought. Yet while some of the language may be at home in a baptismal setting, it is evidently not exclusive to it, and the absence of any unambiguous reference to baptism must lead to caution. Therefore, we shall not be relying on this approach in our interpretation of 1 John's thought. However, it is probable that 1 John uses a variety of confessional and catechetical material from the tradition of the community; the author himself claims to be recalling them to what they already know (1:5; 2:7; 3:11).

It is, then, impossible to understand the thought of 1 John (or any document) without a number of prior decisions, even if only implicit, about its nature as a piece of writing. Yet such decisions can only be made on the basis of the text itself; we are here not relying on early church tradition about the common apostolic authorship of 1 John and the Gospel or about the object of its polemic. The conclusion of this section is that 1 John can be properly treated as a literary unity and so as theologically coherent. It is also not an abstract tract but written to a specific situation, although its theology cannot be reduced to being determined entirely by that situation.

HISTORICAL SETTING

The Third Epistle again offers us the most specific details with which to start an exploration of the situation of the letters. Like 2 John, it is written by someone who can describe himself simply as 'The Elder'. The lack of a personal name is unparalleled in a private letter and offers no guidance as to his possible identification with known figures from the early church. We may assume the title implies a measure of authority since, probably in 3 John and certainly in 2 John, it is used in writing to a church other than the author's own (2 John 13); this would be even more true if in 2 John the author addresses a wider audience than a single church. Thus it is unlikely that the author writes as a member of a college of elders responsible for a local church (as at Acts 20:17) or that the 'title' carries only a note of affectionate respect. Various attempts have been made to associate the title with other uses of it in the early church; in particular some early church writers speak of 'elders' as notable figures who could be looked back to as those who handed on tradition within the church at large rather than holding a defined office (as does Papias in an oft-quoted passage in Eusebius, *Church History* III.39.4). Yet this seems to be a description used by someone else of an earlier authority rather than a title to be claimed by oneself in writing a letter.[13] Other attempts to define his role rely more on interpretations of the situation in an early church setting than on an understanding of the use of 'Elder' (see below, pp. 91–2). If we knew the authority claimed by the author, we might understand better the basis of his dispute with Diotrephes (9–10), but so far no explanation has proved conclusive.

Certainly 3 John implies a wider network than a single community: greetings are sent from and to those identified as 'the friends' (15); the author has attempted, unsuccessfully, to send a letter to 'the church', probably but not certainly Gaius' community; news has been carried by 'the brethren' (3), probably missionaries dependent on the communities for their support (5–8). The author either has some responsibility for these brethren or can be treated as closely linked to them (10). He may envisage visits to the communities to whom he has written, unless these are little more than conventional niceties (10, 14; 2 John 12). Yet how many brethren or communities are involved remains obscure.

Central to 3 John is that the author's authority has been contested; he writes cautiously to Gaius – as indicated by the convoluted grammar of v. 5 – and has been effectively

[13] See the discussion in Lieu, *Second and Third Epistles*, 52–64.

excluded by the unknown Diotrephes (9), whose opposition
has extended even to excluding from the church any who
sought to help the brethren – who themselves share the elder's
opprobrium (10). Such draconian measures imply very serious
points of difference. Most of our parallels to such exclusion
occur in contexts of doctrinal controversy; in 2 John itself those
who fail to bear acceptable teaching are to be denied hospitality, and those who seek to offer it share both the offence and,
probably, the penalty (10–11). If doctrinal issues are at stake
then both their nature and the response of and to exclusion
would be part of the theology of this Epistle. Yet the enigma of
the letter is that no reference is made to such issues, unless in
the assertion that to help such brethren is to be fellow workers
with 'the truth' (8). Neither is Diotrephes labelled as one who
teaches falsely; his faults are to love first place (9) and to be
characteristically one 'who does evil' and who therefore has not
seen God (11).

A fourth figure in the conflict is Demetrius (12); neither his
identity nor his achievements are stated, but presumably he
represents one worthy of imitation, who does do good and has
seen God. Although he is commended not only by the elder but
'by the truth itself', this need not point to any doctrinal fidelity,
for such testimonies have their parallels in purely secular or
civic contexts of those worthy of office or of honour.

We are left with the absence of a clear theological interpretation of a conflict which may none the less have theological
roots. The Elder sees the charges against him only as slander
(10) and as the action of a high-handed autocrat. We may
suspect that Diotrephes has been largely successful both in
retaining the support of the majority (who have not followed
those cast out of the church) and in leaving the Elder with few
counter-measures other than a slightly uncertain 'If I come
…'. This leaves us with a problem in our search for the
theology of the Johannine Epistles. The most apparently
explicit details are contained in 3 John; if it does not stand on
its own but is closely related to the other letters (and to the
Gospel), we might hope it would offer insights into their more
oblique setting. The specific situation may not be identical

with or even similar to that of the other letters, but it must arise from a common theological as well as socio-historical background. Therefore, the initially more obvious solution of dismissing 3 John as too obscure and too brief to offer anything is unsatisfactory. Some attempt must be made to reflect on its ambiguities and on the issues it highlights within a wider Johannine context.[14]

A different situation is implied in 2 John; ostensibly written from within one church to another, this 'letter', as we have seen, may in fact be something more of an open manifesto. Its main concern appears to be the appearance of 'deceivers' whose confession of Jesus Christ is inadequate (7); in response the letter instructs that they are to be excluded from the community, a policy of isolation and not debate (10–11). If the letter were written to a single church we might conclude that it had yet to encounter these deceivers ('If anyone comes ...', 10), but in a manifesto such detail is less reliable. The identity of these deceivers and the exact nature of their error (expressed as a confession they do not make, 7) are something of a problem; it is a problem that should probably not be taken in isolation but only in relation to the similar warning of 1 John 4:2 – which may even be the inspiration of 2 John 7. This means that although grammatically the most natural way of translating their denial would be as a denial of the fleshly parousia of Jesus (that he 'comes' or 'will come in flesh') – thus implying this was part of the theology of our author – the formula is more probably to be interpreted in the light both of 1 John 4:2 (which looks to the past coming of Jesus) and of the description of Jesus as 'the coming one' in the Fourth Gospel (see below, p. 95). Indeed, a number of pointers indicate that 2 John is dependent on 1 John, a dependence to be borne in mind in evaluating its theological contribution.[15]

A common concern of both letters is with travelling teachers; this concern can be well documented in a range of early Christian literature (for instance *Didache* 11). Such travellers, probably not to be strait-jacketed into a single phenomenon, played an important role in the development of the early

---

[14] So Lieu, *Second and Third Epistles.*   [15] *Ibid.*, 76–8, 86.

church but also gave rise to problems and disputes about both their teaching and their authority. They focussed the need to devise measures for assessing acceptable teaching and for treating those found unacceptable; they may also have become a focus of tension in the growth of authority structures within the local church.

In recent years our understanding of such problems has been enriched by a recognition of the social factors and pressures arising from the setting and organisation of the earliest Christian communities. The evidence of the New Testament points to the centrality in that organisation of the 'household' (see 2 John 10), which was already the focal unit in the Graeco-Roman city and which had its own existing pattern of loyalties and obligation.[16] While all this may be only very hazily in the background of 2 and 3 John, we cannot ask about their contribution to the theological response made by the Johannine and New Testament literature without being aware of it.

The very different nature of 1 John demands a different approach to its historical setting. Neither writer nor audience are specified, although a specific situation is implied. The opening verses underline this silence yet also may constitute some claim to authority in the use of the first person plural, 'we', and the language of physical witness. If, as I shall argue, those verses cannot be taken as a simple claim to physical witness of the earthly ministry and particularly the resurrection of Jesus, and so as a guide to the author's identity, they may tell us rather more about the author's views of witness and of tradition.

The audience are equally shadowy; they already know a tradition of Christian preaching, presumably one shared with the author himself (2:7, 24). Whether they belong to a single community, as perhaps implied by 2:19 if taken literally, or to more than one, as possibly indicated by the general lack of particularity, cannot easily be decided. So too, the author's

---

[16] *Ibid.*, 125–35; F. V. Filson, 'The Significance of the Early House Churches', *JBL* 58 (1939), 105–12.

precise relationship with them remains unclear; he writes to them and yet claims a close identity with them.

What does seem secure is the fact of recent schism and the crisis it has created for the community. The first explicit reference to this comes half way through the letter in 2:19, which tells us only that 'they went out from us'; the same people must be in mind in 4:1f., which speaks of the false prophets who have gone out into the world and which is linked to 2:18–22 by a concern for the right confession of Jesus and by the term 'the antichrist' (4:3). As we shall see, the language of 'antichrist' and 'false prophets' tells us little about their behaviour or views and rather more about the author's interpretation of them as harbingers of the final age. While these references imply schism, 2:26 warns against 'those who are' or perhaps 'are trying to deceive you', as does 3:7. This implies some continuing relationship or dialogue, and it is not clear whether the separation is as absolute as the author would like.[17]

The fault of these 'schismatics' is expressed as a matter of failure regarding christological confession (2:22; 4:2–3), a failure which is important for what it tells us about the author's positive concerns but which also invites attempts to identify this with known christological conflicts within the early church.

Besides the explicit attack against those who fail to make the right confession, much of the letter, starting already in 1:6, is concerned with the correlation between claims to have fellowship with God, to know him, to be in the light, and practical behaviour as manifested in keeping commands, loving a brother or doing sin. Despite the fact that these issues are not debated with direct reference to the schismatics, the dominant interpretation of the letter has assumed that they are part of the same conflict. Thus it is widely accepted that the debating, antithetical style is a polemical one, and that the claims or the claim/behaviour mismatches which are rejected can be

[17] P. Perkins, *The Johannine Epistles* (Dublin, 1980), xxii–xxiii emphasises the rhetorical nature of the language and warns against taking it too literally as a reflection of the actual historical situation.

assigned to the schismatics and used to profile and identify them. What the author rejects is what they claimed or did. It has then been common to correlate the christological and 'moral' aspects of the debate in order to provide the schismatics with a coherent ideology.[18]

The imprecision of the letter has inevitably led to an imprecise and varied depiction of the schismatics. A minority position has been that the opponents are 'Jewish–Christian', unable to accept the messiahship of Jesus as understood by our author.[19] For most studies a common thread has been their focus on the divine element within Jesus Christ to the detriment of a clear understanding of the saving significance of his human experience (that he was 'in flesh' (4:2)), and a corresponding sense of their present possession of knowledge of God and freedom from sin regardless of their actual behaviour and attitude to one another. In broad outline this picture betrays similarities with a 'gnostic' position with its devaluation of the material world, denial that the Redeemer could be fully identified with the material ('flesh'), and (as reported by the church opponents) libertine life-style. The vagueness of detail in 1 John and the absence of any reference to the other aspects of a gnostic position has led most scholars to speak of the opponents of 1 John as proto-gnostic or 'on the way'. The failure to take seriously the humanity of Jesus does have its parallels in the early church; Ignatius writing around CE 110 had met such docetic views in the churches of Asia Minor, but his letters imply a far more precise articulation than we could draw from 1 John. Others have pointed to the, probably legendary, conflict between John the disciple of the Lord and Cerinthus reported by the early church. According to later reports Cerinthus saw the union between the divine and human in Jesus Christ as only temporary, initiated at the baptism and finishing with the departure of the divine 'Christ'

---

[18] Most commentaries conduct such an exercise in their introductions; see also J. Painter, 'The "Opponents" in 1 John', *NTS* 32 (1986), 48–71 and below, pp. 75–7.

[19] So O'Neill, *Puzzle of 1 John*; S. S. Smalley, *1, 2, 3 John*, Word Biblical Commenatry (Waco, 1984), xiii–xv, argues for two schismatic groups, one of which is Jewish–Christian.

before the crucifixion, thus avoiding the participation of the divine in suffering. Yet Cerinthus too seems to have followed a more developed system than that known by 1 John. The evidence is not provided by 1 John to identify the opponents' position with these more articulated systems, and it is probable that they did not represent a 'system' as such.

Acknowledging this, many scholars have been concerned to trace the possible origin of the views held by these opponents. We shall see later that the Fourth Gospel can be read as emphasising the divinity more greatly than the humanity of Jesus; thus a number of studies, well represented by R. Brown, have argued that their views could have arisen from a particular (and perhaps one-sided) reading of the Gospel.[20]

I shall not elaborate this sketch in any more detail, but its consequences for interpreting 1 John's theology should be noted. If 1 John's thought is primarily polemical, it is best understood in contrast to the views it opposes and as not necessarily a balanced statement; the author's silences may be equally polemical or defensive. The debating style as well as the dualistic thought of the letter may be as much a function of the polemic in which it is engaged as a key structure in the author's theology. If the author is writing in conscious awareness of the Fourth Gospel and against those who also claimed to interpret that Gospel, the Fourth Gospel can hardly be ignored in any exposition of the letter's thought. As we have already seen in relation to the previous section, the fact that the letter's literary nature is open to more than one interpretation means a prior decision about it has to be made before the letter can be interpreted, even if we are trying to explore its internal theology as a single text.

The approach taken here, which will be repeated and tested in the course of the study, is that, however serious the schism, the polemic against specific views and claims of opponents does not control the letter or its thought. The so-called 'moral debate' is not explicitly related to the schismatics and so should not be interpreted purely as a reaction against them. To

---

[20] See also, J. L. Houlden, *A Commentary on the Johannine Epistles* (London, 1973), 17–20, but also allowing for external influences.

use the debate to reconstruct their beliefs and then to use their reconstructed beliefs to interpret the debate demands a circularity of argument which is only justified if other approaches fail. So too their relation to the Fourth Gospel should not be assumed independently of a wider consideration of the relationship between the Epistle and the Gospel. The author's failure to spell out his opponents' views and to refute them must be taken seriously – they are not his chief concern. The structure and rhetoric of the letter suggest that while the fact and impact of the schism can hardly be denied – although it may be difficult to separate out fact from interpretation in 2:18–22 and 4:1–3 – its chief result has been to engender a debate within the framework of the author's or community's theology. The recognition that the 'opponents'' views could have developed from the Fourth Gospel is due to the fact that they are potential elements within the author's own 'Johannine' theology. The antithetical, debating style is all part of the thought and theological pattern of 1 John. Moreover, since on the basis of the christological debate alone little advance can be made as to the views of the opponents – and after all, we have only the author's own perspective – little is to be gained by the use of such labels as 'gnostic' or, of 1 John, 'anti-gnostic'.[21] It is therefore possible and necessary to explore the theology of the letter without immediate and prior reference to the views of its opponents.

THE JOHANNINE BACKGROUND

Numerous parallels of language, style and theology unite the Second and Third with the First Epistle and all three with the Gospel of John. Whereas at one time common authorship of all four writings was assumed, it is now more widely thought that the Epistles should be attributed to a different author (or

---

[21] It is often argued that images possibly stemming from the letter's opponents, such as 'anointing' (2:20, 27) or 'seed' (3:9), have gnostic overtones; while this may make 1 John 'anti-gnostic', some of the letter's own images, such as being born from God, have also been labelled 'gnostic'. These labels are used so loosely, without relation to a total structure of thought that might justify them, that they serve little purpose.

authors) from the Gospel. Another less certain member of the Johannine corpus is the Revelation of St John, which does share with the others some characteristics of language but whose apocalyptic outlook appears to belong to the opposite end of the spectrum to that of the Gospel and letters.

Modern study of the Gospel finds in it signs of earlier sources and/or stages of development, if not also of later editing. John 21:24 clearly suggests that the author was not a solitary figure but was accompanied or followed by others who were able to, and saw a need to, set a seal of approval on his Gospel. If we add to this the separate authorship of the Epistles, we must think of a number of contributors whose work is marked by a general unity of outlook, that is of what may be termed a 'Johannine school'.[22] However we envisage this as working in practice, it means that the telling of the story of Jesus and the reflecting on it evidenced by the Gospel were carried on by more than one person and perhaps handed on from one to the next. Within this we may think of certain leading figures – the 'Elder' of 2 and 3 John, the 'I' of 1 John, and perhaps at an early stage the shadowy person represented by the Beloved Disciple in the Gospel; we should perhaps think too of a group – the 'we' of John 21:24 and possibly of the prologue of 1 John. Yet to none of these figures can we put a name.

We have already seen that the Epistles imply more than one community owing some loyalty to the Johannine tradition. The language of the Gospel too seems to be aimed at an audience for whom its pattern of thought and enigmatic images – such as being born again (John 3) – would be more familiar than for the perplexed outsider. Thus behind the Johannine literature we may picture communities of Christians for whom the Johannine way of expression was familiar and from whose wider deposit of tradition the Gospel and Epistles have drawn.

The lack of clear internal information has led to considerable debate as to the origins of the distinctive Johannine Christianity. Parallels in the Gospel, and more so in 1 John, with the

[22] The concept of a 'school' is well explored in relation to other groupings in the ancient world by R. A. Culpepper, *The Johannine School*, SBLDS 26 (Missoula, 1975).

Qumran writings have led modern scholarship to trace its origins in so-called 'sectarian Judaism'. However, our ignorance about the full variety of forms of Jewish thought in and outside Palestine should make us hesitate before locating the beginnings of Johannine thought too precisely. Undoubtedly both the Gospel and First Epistle are the outcome of a lengthy process of development within Johannine thought. References within the Gospel have led many to isolate significant stages in this development including the influx of 'heterodox' Jews or Samaritans (see John 4), the exclusion of 'Johannine Christians' from the Jewish synagogue (John 9:22; 12:42; 16:2), and possibly the advent of Gentiles (John 12:20). In this way the Gospel is seen as telling the story of Jesus through the mirror or prism of the community's own experiences.[23] So, for example, the Gospel's hostility against the Jews is likely to reflect contemporary or recent conflict with the Jewish community, and it is notable that issues such as Sabbath observance take second place to the status of Jesus as Son of God (see John 5:9–18), which is recognised as posing a real threat to Jewish monotheism. Others have told a theological history of the community by drawing on the distinct perspectives of supposed layers of sources and editing.[24] Both methods treat the Gospel as a tell exposed by an archaeological survey whose several layers of occupation reveal the history of its occupants.

Many of such surveys have presented the Epistles as a further stage in the history, sometimes as a stage which contains the clues for identifying earlier stages. We have already encountered some of the reasons for this in looking at

[23] A number of scholars have done this following the work of J. L. Martyn, *History and Theology in the Fourth Gospel* (New York, 1979); see also R. E. Brown, *The Community of the Beloved Disciple* (New York and London, 1979). How far a Gospel can be used as an archaeological site for this purpose is a matter of dispute, but that the Gospel does reflect recent experience does seem likely.

[24] So, for example, A. J. Mattill, jr. 'Johannine Communities behind the Fourth Gospel', *TS* 38 (1977), 294–315 offers an English summary of the views of G. Richter, found in 'Die Fleischwerdung des Logos im Johannesevangelium', *NovT* 13 (1971), 81–126; 14 (1972), 257–76 and other articles; see also J. Painter, 'The Farewell Discourses and the History of Johannine Christianity', *NTS* 27 (1981), 525–43; H. Thyen, 'Entwicklungen innerhalb der johanneischen Theologie und Kirche im Spiegel von Joh 21 und der Lieblingsjüngertexte des Evangeliums', in M. de Jonge (ed.), *L'Evangile de Jean*, BETL 44 (Gembloux, 1977), 259–99.

the literary nature of 1 John and its relation with the Gospel, and in exploring the polemical setting of the same letter. In particular it has been noted that 1 John makes no mention of the issues at stake in the controversy with 'the Jews', although the confession of Jesus as 'the Christ' or Son of God is a key problem. Its concerns are more inwardly directed, although the inner unity of the community may well be equally although less explicitly at issue in the Gospel (John 17). However, a minority view – recently growing – has preferred to see 1 John as prior to the Gospel, or as independent of it so that the two represent separate 'crystallisations' of the Johannine tradition in different circumstances.

To decide the question we have no external evidence, although it may be that 1 John was accepted more easily and sooner than the Gospel by the wider church.[25] Since the Gospel is a single text and not visibly layered in the manner of a tell, any reconstruction can only appeal to the texts themselves and to the careful reader's sensitivity towards the texts. Decisions about sequence are inseparable from decisions about what is going on behind the Epistle and Gospel, and about the probable sequence of such events in the life of a community. In fact these decisions are far more complex than often realised, and in this study of the Epistles we shall acknowledge the wider Johannine setting and yet avoid using the Gospel to elaborate or to settle uncertainties of interpretation. No particular sequence between Gospel and Epistles is being assumed, nor, as has been stated, is any particular reconstruction of the linking historical events. It will be clear from what has already been said that this position is no more neutral than any other!

However, if the Johannine writings come from a wider setting, from communities with a distinctive history and tradition of theology, there must be a tension between the contribution of the individual author and that of the community. It would be wrong simply to identify the theology of any one or all of these writings with that of the community. This is

---

[25] Either 1 John or its language is known by Polycarp, while in the Muratorian canon, perhaps dating from the end of the second century, it does seem that 1 John is being cited to buttress the authority of the Gospel.

often done when conclusions have been drawn from the Johannine writings as to the form and structure or the self-understanding of the Johannine communities. Yet the author may be adopting, modifying or correcting the tradition of his community as well as making his own individual and creative contribution. On the other hand, everything that has been said so far about context and setting points to the importance of recognising the role played by the community.

Besides the background provided by the particular setting of the letters, and the tradition of Johannine thought, the antecedents of that thought in Judaism and /or Hellenism are also important. What images or framework did the authors or first readers bring with them which would colour their understanding of the texts? Again we have no other evidence than that provided by the Gospel and Epistles themselves and here there have been sharp swings in fashion; the Gospel has been interpreted as profoundly Hellenistic, but now its antecedents in Judaism, albeit 'Hellenistic Judaism', have been increasingly recognised. Something similar has happened with the Epistles. Admittedly the names and dominant conventions of 3 John are Greek, and some of the dictinctive terms and images of 1 John ('anointing', 'seed', becoming like him on seeing him, 3:2) have been seen as evidence of a more Hellenistic setting than that of the Gospel.[26] Allied to this have been views, referred to above, of 1 John as 'gnostic' even while it is attacking 'gnostic' ideas. Yet in many respects 1 John can now be set against a background in a Judaism such as that of the Dead Sea Scrolls, particularly in its dualism – indeed there have been attempts to claim for it knowledge of or even the origin of its 'source' in such sectarian Judaism.[27] While this may be going too far, we shall see that 1 John's apparent disregard for the Old Testament is deceptive, and the Jewish parallels offer useful insights into the letter. Obviously, however, the dominant explicit background is the Christian

[26] So C. H. Dodd, *The Johannine Epistles* (London, 1946), lii–liii.
[27] See the essays in J. H. Charlesworth, *John and Qumran* (London, 1972) (and ch. 2, pp. 82–3 below), and the theory of O'Neill, *Puzzle of 1 John*, that 1 John is a reworking of a sectarian Jewish document.

background: it is this which the author assumes. He does not address his readers as converts from anything, but as those who have heard 'from the beginning'. His own starting point is the same certainty.

Finally we must ask whether there is a wider Christian background to the Epistles. In theory it may be hard to picture a form of Christianity untouched by any other, especially if we are to date the Epistles to the end of the first century. (This is often done, although the evidence is completely open and much depends on the relationship with the Gospel.) In 2 and 3 John there may be links with Pauline tradition, particularly in the greeting of 2 John and some of the 'mission' language of 3 John.[28] Such links cannot be read back into the larger Epistle. In 1 John there are some parallels with Matthaean traditions, but it seems most likely that these only reflect its sharing in some of the basic kerygma behind the rest of New Testament Christianity, something that is hardly surprising.[29] However, since such relationships as these are are not on the conscious or reactive level, we are fully justified in now exploring the theology of the Johannine Epistles in their own terms.

[28] See Lieu, *Second and Third Epistles*, 47, 106–7.
[29] These parallels are set out by Dodd in *Epistles*, xxxviii–vlii, and explained as due to use of a body of traditional sayings of Jesus; O. A. Piper, '1 John and the Didache of the Primitive Church', *JBL* 66 (1947), 437–51 explores the links with basic NT teaching more generally.

CHAPTER 2

The theology of the Johannine Epistles

The First Epistle of John has often been likened to a spiral;
again and again it returns to a point where it has been before,
and yet by bringing in a new element moves on a step further.
This spiral is not merely a technique of literary style and structure, but is equally an expression of thought-structure.
Inevitably, then, its theology cannot be separated out topic by
topic; themes and ideas are interwoven, and it is impossible to
explore one without having to say something about the others
as well. This means that to present 1 John's theology through
the stages of an argument would be to misrepresent it. Yet the
letter does offer some hints as to a starting point. Its purpose is
not first of all to engage in polemic with outsiders or with their
views, and so we shall not start, as is often done, from the points
where the author disagrees with his supposed opponents.
Instead its purpose is stated explicitly at the beginning and at
the effective end of the letter – the proclamation and assurance
of eternal life (1:2; 5:13; the theme is repeated at the very end of
the letter in 5:20). The concept of 'Eternal Life' constitutes the
basic framework of the letter with the promise of its presence
repeated at the focal point of the letter after the first introduction of the schismatics – it is both the basis and the goal of
remaining faithful (2:25).[1] Eternal life also holds together the
past – for it is that which was manifested or given (1:2; 5:11) –
and the present – as that which is proclaimed and is experienced (1:2; 5:13). As these same key verses show, it also holds
together the readers' commitment to the past, expressed in
right belief, and the assurance they have in the present (2:23,

[1] 'Eternal life' comes only at 1 John 1:2; 2:25; 5:11,13,20 and at 3:15.

22

where denying or confessing the Son is the precondition of (not) having the Father, prepares for 2:25, while 5:12, where the one who has the Son has life, leads into 5:13). These then form the centre of the spiral – and so of the theology of 1 John – the eternal life that is known, and how it may be known; the letter is marked not by argument but by certainty and exhortation, by what is the case and how it might be proved to be the case. Again, with reference to both past and present, to assurance and testing, this refers not to abstract or general truth but to them, the readers; 1 John is guided less by argument than by its use of 'you' (plural) and even more of 'we' (which appears more times in 1 John than any other NT letter of comparable length).[2] This, the author and the community, his use of 'we' and 'you', offers a starting point for 1 John's theology.

THE AUTHOR AND THE COMMUNITY

The author of 1 John preserves his anonymity, but it is not only this which makes him such a shadowy figure; his presentation of himself through his letter is full of ambiguity. At first, it is true, the opening verses of 1 John seem to claim an unequivocal authority. '*You*', the readers, are sharply distinguished from '*we*' who proclaim and write. 'You' are the recipients of a letter and of a proclamation; the authority of the letter and of its writer is that of one who can say 'we have heard ... seen with our eyes ... our hands have touched' (1:1). This sounds like the priority claimed by an eyewitness, if not of the whole ministry of Jesus, then surely of his death and resurrection. Yet a second reading makes the eyewitness claim less obvious. That which was heard, seen and handled is not Jesus, the Son, or even 'the Word who was in the beginning' (cf. John 1:1), but 'that [thing:neuter] which was from the beginning ... concerning the word of life' (v. 1). It was life, not Jesus, which was

---

[2] 'You' comes less frequently in 1 John (34 occasions) than in James (39) or 1 Peter (51), but in them the genitive ('your') dominates, whereas in 1 John it is the dative ('to you'). 'We (us, our)' comes 53 times in the Johannine Epistles, exceeded only by Romans (59) 1 Cor. (54) and 2 Cor. (108).

manifested (v. 1). There is little in the letter as a whole to suggest the work of an eyewitness of Jesus, and later the community itself can be ascribed a similar witness experience (4:14,16). Those who ascribe 1 John to a later author than the Gospel have a further reason for doubting the literal intention of any eyewitness claim in 1 John 1:1–4. Most would see in that neuter a reference instead to the preaching which makes available the original witness experience. Yet if the author was not himself a literal eyewitness, it is more, not less, significant that the ultimate authority he wishes to claim for his letter lies not in the terms we meet elsewhere in the New Testament – apostle, slave of Jesus Christ, brother of ... – but in the anonymous authority of witness. It is an authority which is not individual – although elsewhere the letter speaks only of a single author, here it speaks of 'we'. Perhaps the author, not literally an eyewitness of Jesus' ministry, uses the language of eye- and earwitness in virtue of his place within a group which saw itself as standing in continuity with the first witnesses and as maintaining the continuity and unity of the tradition rooted in that witness.[3] A similar awareness may lie behind John 1:18. In view of the parallels in the Gospel (also 3:11; see 1:34), he may be quoting (vv. 1–2) and then applying (3–4) formulaic language of the community.

The task of the witness in these opening verses is not 'to hand on' (contrast 1 Cor. 15:1–3; 11:23) but to proclaim. It would be easy to conclude from this that the readers had not yet heard the things to be proclaimed; the author speaks with an almost prophetic authority out of his ('our') experience to their need to hear.[4] Yet this is a note which the rest of the letter fails to sustain. He does indeed speak to his readers as 'children' (2:1,18, 28; 3:18), as a teacher might to his pupils (cf. Sir. 3:1; 4:1 etc.), or as 'beloved' (2:7; 4:1,7), which need not carry the note of intimacy it does for us since it can belong to the

---

[3] For example R. Schnackenburg, *Die Johannesbriefe* (Freiburg, 1979), 52–8.
[4] That the author speaks from different 'roles' and here does so as prophet was argued by E. Lohmeyer, 'Über Aufbau und Gliederung des ersten Johannesbriefes', *ZNW* 27 (1928), 226–63.

exhortations of testament literature.[5] He does also command
them (2:28; 4:1) and give an authoritative interpretation of
recent events (2:18f.) and of Christian practice (5:16–17). Yet
alongside these notes of a spiritual authority exercised from
above or outside stand others which place the author within
the community, if not literally, then in spirit. His individual
identity becomes absorbed in that of the community as a whole
and of each member. The first person singular, 'I', is used only
with the verb 'to write' – 'I am writing'/'I wrote' – otherwise
the author claims no other individual and independent activity
for himself than the assertive plural claim of the opening
verses. Even that claim is one that can also be made for all
members of the community, corporately and not individually.
In 1 John 4:12–16 it is 'we' who love one another, who
experience the indwelling of God and of his love, who have
received the gift of the holy spirit, who also 'have seen and bear
witness that the Father sent his Son as saviour of the world'
and who 'have known and put their faith in the love which God
had for us'. Here 'we' must be the whole community, who,
because of their experience of God's love and gifts, and indeed
of mutual indwelling with God, can use the language of witness
themselves. No doubt they could use it only because some did
physically see and believe; probably, too, that initial awareness
of sight and experience was maintained as a continuing vital
ingredient within the community's life. If, as the opening
verses suggest, authority was rooted not in appointed or
inherited roles but in that awareness of witness, it must have
been seen as an authority not limited to certain individuals
(although it may have been predicated particularly of them),
but potentially available to every member of the community.

Authority, then, even if claimed by the author, is not
exclusive to him or to a restricted circle; that, grounded in the
life and belief of the community, it is available to every member
is something that becomes apparent in other ways. He may
address them as children, but he acknowledges that they have
no need of a teacher (2:27), for they have an anointing which

5 So K. Berger, 'Apostelbrief und apostolische Rede, Zum Formular frühchristlicher
  Brief', *ZNW* 65 (1974), 190–231, 212.

teaches them about everything.[6] He can claim little for himself that cannot be said of the community: 'he' ('we') has heard (1:3, 5), but so have they; 'we' bear witness, and so do they (1:2; 4:12); 'we' have fellowship with the Father and the Son (1:3 – the purpose of writing is that they may have fellowship with 'us'), but so apparently do they claim fellowship with 'him' (God?) (1:6). In all this the author has no priority over the community.

Although in the opening verses 'we' stand over against 'you', for most of the letter 'we' denotes not the author and his fellow authorities, an exclusive circle, but the community together with the author. Together they deliberate the authenticity of their own religious claims and how such claims might be proved invalid: 'If we say that we have fellowship with him and walk in darkness, we deceive ourselves and do not do the truth' (1:6). By the contrasting of false with authentic correlations between claims and behaviour, a true path can be mapped: 'By this we know that we have known him, if we keep his commands' (2:3). This might, of course, be not genuine debate but rhetorical persuasiveness; perhaps the author seeks to convince his readers by inviting them into a process of deliberation whose conclusions are as inevitable as they are implicit in the starting point he has chosen. The same rhetoric may be at play when he confidently asserts what 'we' know (3:2). Yet even if this is rhetoric and not open debate, it betrays no authoritarian control by the author. He appeals to no other grounds of external authority to buttress his position. He cannot add to his armoury the weight of his own standing, of private revelation, of spiritual power, of access to independent tradition or scriptural precedent. Even if our author is not genuinely engaged in corporate deliberation with the community, he can do no other than adopt the guise of being so. He may indeed be seeking to win them over to a confidence they do not possess when he affirms their assured knowledge (5:18–19), but that assurance is always 'ours' or 'yours' and never 'mine'.

---

[6] See below, pp. 28–9 on the 'anointing'. In 2.20 there is some textual uncertainty as to whether the text should read 'and you all know' or 'and you know all'.

So, too, he may address them as 'you' and even command or exhort them (4:1), yet more frequently 'you' is used in affirmations underlining what they already possess or know (4:4). Wherever there is a command there is always not very far away a strong affirmation to soften its impact (2:15 following 2:12–14; 2:28 following 2:27). Where more serious issues are at stake the author uses an indirect impersonal third person singular, 'He who ... ', 'Everyone who ... ' (2:9–11; 3:4–10). Certainly there are serious issues, but his approach to them is more co-operative than directive. Whatever the historical reality of the situation, the relationship between author and community in 1 John is not that of spiritual founder and infant church, or of disciplining teacher responsible for an erring congregation, but of a community at once confident in their assurance and yet engaged in the process of deliberation about the consequences of that assurance in a situation where there is no external yardstick by which to measure themselves. The author, perhaps in reality outside the situation and by the very act of writing claiming to interpret it, can only share in it and recognise their own independence of him (2:12–14).

For 1 John authority lies within the life and experience of the believing community; finding the way forward is a shared enterprise, and examination of their present Christian life is done from within and not from outside.

'WE KNOW': CONFIDENCE IN THE LIFE OF THE COMMUNITY

Although the community of 1 John need vigilance because of those who might deceive them (2:26), must exercise sincere and practical love (3:18), and are urged to test the spirits (4:1), the over-riding sense is of the assurance of what they already know, have achieved, possess and are. Although he exhorts and encourages (2:15), he writes because their sins *are* forgiven, they *do* have knowledge of the one from the beginning and the Father, they *have* conquered, *are* strong and *do* experience God's indwelling word (2:12–14). Victory is already theirs, over the evil one, over those who would oppose them, and over the world (4:4; 5:4f.). This is the eternal life which we saw forms the backbone of the letter. Life, knowledge, victory, strength are 'eschatological' realities; elsewhere in the New Testament they belong in full to the final defeat of evil and realisation of God's kingdom.[7] For 1 John they are part of the community's present experience and a key to their confidence. The reverse side to this is the portrayal of those who left the community: appearing now in the present, they are the manifestation of the forces of opposition to God who belong to the final times (2:18; 4:1). In resisting them the community share in the ultimate victory of those who belong to God.

The confidence they have is expressed in various ways; at its heart is knowledge – although, as in John, it is the verb ('to know') and not the noun ('knowledge') which is used. Believers 'know' both theological truths ('he was manifest to take away sin', 3:5; also 2:29; 5:20) and religious certainties ('we have passed from death to life', 3:14; also 5:13,15,18,19 etc.) As in this last example, what 'we' know is what is already the case – that we have passed, (we) have eternal life, the Son of God has given us understanding, God does hear us, we are of God ... The only future object of knowledge – that 'we shall be like him' – is rooted in what is already true, that 'we are children of God' (3:2).

To 'know' is also the purpose of the testing of confidence – 'By this we *know* that we have known him, if ... ' (2:3f.; 3:19; 5:2). Appropriate behaviour confirms the believers' self-awareness or knowledge, as does the experience of the spirit (3:24; 4:13). In fact, knowledge of what God has done or will do (the theological truths) is far less significant than the self-knowledge regarding their own, demonstrable, standing as believers.

Believers also simply 'know' – they know the truth, they are taught concerning all things and so they all 'know' (2:21,27,20).[8] They have no need of a teacher or of further illumination, but only of continuing in what, or in the one who, is already theirs (2:27). Here the source of this knowledge is the 'anointing' (*charisma*) which they have received from the holy

[7] See Luke 11:22; 18:18,30; 1 Cor. 13:9,12; Rev. 15:2; 21:6–7.   [8] See n. 6 above.

one or from 'him' (2:20,27). This term, which does not come
elsewhere in the New Testament, can refer either to an action
or to that which is used – to the anointing or to the oil or
ointment. In 1 John it might be meant literally, referring to a
rite within the church (perhaps baptism or a rite using oil),[9] or
spiritually/metaphorically. If, as seems likely since the anointing is to 'remain in you', the emphasis is on that which is used
and received, it has been taken as referring to the holy spirit
and its activity, to the word of God, or to the initial teaching, or
catachesis, leading to baptism. The novelty of the term has led
some to suggest that the author is introducing a term which
was used by his (gnostic) opponents – perhaps they claimed a
superior knowledge given in a particular rite; he counters with
the assertion that all believers know all that is necessary,
whether through the spirit or through baptismal teaching.[10]
However, since the author can also speak of the 'anti*christ*',
'*chris*ma' is probably a term which he himself has coined or
which comes from the tradition of his own community.

One explanation of the background of the idea is that just as
Jesus was 'anointed' with the spirit (Acts 10:38; Luke 4:18; Isa.
61:1), here believers are similarly anointed, and through their
individual spirit possession have no need of an earthly teacher.[11] Within the community of 1 John this, it is suggested,
resulted in the spirit-awareness of each individual being taken
to excess, leading to unacceptable forms of behaviour and
teaching and so to schism and thence to the call to test the
spirits (4:1–4). However, since 1 John does use the term 'spirit'
– it is the proof of God's abiding presence in the believer and a
source of confession (3:24; 4:2,13) – it would be strange for him
to use a different term here for the same reality. The context
here has to do with knowledge and with teaching; the anointing must abide in believers in the same way as 'what you have

---

[9] That 1 John refers to a rite of 'unction' is argued by W. Nauck, *Die Tradition und der
Charakter*, 155–9, and, with caution, by T. W. Manson, 'Entry into Membership of
the Early Church', *JTS* 48 (1947), 25–33,29; both authors note the tradition of
anointing preceding baptism in the Syriac church.

[10] See Grayson, *Epistles*, 84–8.

[11] On this and what follows see G. M. Burge, *The Anointed Community. The Holy Spirit in
the Johannine Tradition* (Michigan, 1987), 172–3.

heard from the beginning' (2:24). (It is true that in John 14:17 and 26 the spirit both is a source of teaching and will abide in and with the disciples, but this should not be read into our passage, where the parallel with 2:24 seems more significant.) Rather than the community's confidence being essentially 'charismatic', the spirit can pose problems (4:1f.); it is the received teaching or tradition which is more likely to be at the heart of their confidence.

Continuity with the tradition which went back to the beginning of their existence is part of the authenticity of where they now stand (2:7,24; 3:11; cf. 2 John 5,6); this too is what they have held or heard, and so implicitly what they know. In 1:1 'that which was from the beginning' may refer not to the beginning of time (as in John 1:1) but to the beginning of the community's existence, either in the ministry of Jesus or its foundation;[12] as we have seen, the neuter 'that' linked with 'concerning the word of life' draws attention to the proclamation which makes present the original experience of faith. The appeal has been seen as an appeal to their baptismal confession, but the language is not exclusively baptismal. We are less aware of the content of 'what is from the beginning' than that allegiance to it is essential if they are to continue as faithful believers (2:24). Yet it forms the mainstay of the author's argument. It is from here that he starts (1:5); to proceed he can only remind them of the command which they already have 'from the beginning' (2:7; 3:11); the present schism can only be interpreted by what they have already heard (2:18; 4:3) – although in each case the conclusions he draws may be new. Yet this looking back should not be labelled 'tradition'; their identity and confidence lie not in a tradition to be received and passed on, but in something heard and proclaimed. We might want to speak of a kerygmatic community rather than a charismatic one.

There are not two separate sources of confidence or two

---

[12] See Lieu, *Second and Third Epistles*, 173–4; I. de la Potterie, 'La Notion de 'commencement' dans les ecrits Johanniques', in *Die Kirche des Anfangs*, ed. R. Schnackenburg et al. (Freiburg and Leipzig, 1978), 379–403, 396f., argues for the beginning of Jesus' revelation to his disciples.

aspects of religious experience here, namely the present victory won *and* that which they have heard from the beginning. The two combine as a single truth – in 2:14 the 'young men' are strong *and* the word of God abides in them *and* they have conquered the evil one. In 1 John the 'word of God' is not a christological title; it is that which one keeps or has heard, just as is the commandment (2:5–7); it is that which abides in believers (1:10; 2:14). If what was from the beginning abides in them, then so will they abide in the Son and the Father (2:24). The strong 'realised' or present religious experience of 1 John is rooted in the believers' fidelity to, and participation in, the tradition and life of the community. Although the language of religious experience – birth from God, mutual indwelling with God – may sound highly individualistic, that of faithfulness to what has been seen, heard and witnessed is corporate. Confidence belongs to the community.

This theme of confidence is such a central feature of 1 John that it could be explored in a number of directions; because each direction would take us into a significant area of the thought of 1 John, they can best be discussed individually.

'FELLOWSHIP WITH HIM': THE LANGUAGE OF RELIGIOUS EXPERIENCE

The images which dominate 1 John are those of what each believer already possesses or is; the primary tenses are present and perfect. Many of the images do not lend themselves easily to exhortation to further striving or to warning against back-sliding or incompleteness. This is true even though a funda-mental theme of the letter is that where appropriate behaviour, chiefly the exercise of mutual love, is missing, claims to religious experience are by definition null and void. That such claims can be made is not disputed; neither is there any suggestion that those who have left the community meant something different by them than those who remain. Explor-ation of the different images helps give shape to the overall thought patterns of 1 John and provokes the question from where these ideas come and how they are intended. Most of these images are of what believers 'do' or are; for want of a better term we shall speak of 'religious experience',[13] but this does not mean that the author has our modern concern for the individual's inner world. We cannot move with confidence from the type of language to the author's or readers' psychological experience.

Knowing him

That 'we have known him' is a true characteristic of believers, though it must be proved by obedience to his commands (2:3–4; 4:7–8). At times it is clear that it is God who is or has been known (2:14; 4:6–8). Elsewhere the object of knowledge is more ambiguous; in 2:13–14 'the one from the beginning' is perhaps more likely to be Jesus, with an emphasis on the proclamation about him which is the foundation of the community. Most frequently the one known is 'him' (in Greek the personal pronoun *auton*), and the context does not always let us decide for certain between God or Jesus (2:3–4; 3:1. The conjunction with having 'seen' him in 3:6 may point to Jesus). This ambiguous use of 'him' is characteristic of 1 John (see below, pp. 72–3), but need not mean that the distinction between Father and Son has been blurred or that we should talk of knowledge of God 'in the Son'.[14]

As in the Fourth Gospel, where knowing God is equally important and is the goal of the coming of the Son (compare 1 John 5:20 with John 17:3),[15] knowledge denotes relationship rather than factual knowledge or a perception of reality. This is equally true in the Old Testament, where knowledge of God involves acknowledgement, confession and obedience (Jer. 31:33–4); it belongs to the covenant relationship with God.[16] It

---

13 E. Malatesta, *Interiority and Covenant*, AnBib 69 (Rome, 1978), speaks of 'interiority' as the key theme of 1 John.

14 Contrast Smalley, *1, 2, 3 John*, 45, 47.

15 1 John 5:20 comes from the community tradition, as is shown by the introductory 'tradition' word 'we know' (Greek *oidamen*) and by the parallel with John 17:3; both passages speak of knowing God as 'the true', which is only otherwise used in 1 John of the light (2:8).

16 M. E. Boismard, 'La Connaissance de l'alliance nouvelle, d'après la première lettre de saint Jean', *RB* 56 (1949), 365–91, 388f. argues that 1 John consciously sees

is even more true in the Qumran literature, where knowledge is at the heart of God's revelation to the individual – 'Thou hast given me knowledge through thy marvellous mysteries' (1QH 11:9). At Qumran knowledge is vouchsafed only to the members of the community and is inseparable from obedience to God's requirements as made known to the community (1QS 9:16–19). However, 1 John never develops a covenant framework, and instead knowledge of God belongs to a complex of other expressions of religious experience which have fewer parallels in Jewish thought. For this reason the Johannine affinity for 'knowing' is sometimes labelled 'gnostic', allying it with those systems of second-century (and later) thought at the heart of which stood the individual's enlightenment or acquisition of esoteric knowledge. There, however, knowledge is in contrast to ignorance or error (as in the *Gospel of Truth* 16.39, 'the salvation of those who were ignorant of the Father'; 22.13f., 'he who possesses knowledge knows whence he is come and whither he is going'); this is a theme foreign to 1 John as it is to John. In 1 John it is the one who does (not) love who has (not) known God; the meaning of 'love' or of 'keeping his commands' (4:7–8; 2:3f.) is crucial for understanding the framework within which 1 John's thought moves (see below, pp. 66–71).

Born of God; children of God

In the second part of 1 John a key theme is that believers are born of God (3:9; 4:7; 5:1,4,18) or are children of God (3:1f.,10; 5:2). Here the author uses a different word for 'children' of God (*tekna*) from when he addresses his readers as 'children' (*teknia, paidia*: 2:1; 12,28; 3:7,18; 4:4; 5:21; 2:14,18).[17] As *children*, believers do not share the same status as the Son (*huios*) (in contrast to Paul, who can use 'son' of both Jesus and Chris-

---

'knowledge of God' as the fulfilment of the new covenant hope of Jeremiah and Ezekiel; I shall argue that the absence of explicit covenant language is against this.

[17] The same distinction is followed in the Gospel: 'children of God' or 'children of Abraham' (1:12; 11:52; 8:39) uses *tekna*, but Jesus addresses his disciples as *teknia* or *paidia* (13:33; 21:5). In contrast 2 and 3 John only use *tekna* – of members of the community (2 John 1,4,13; 3 John 4).

tians), but they owe their status not to adoption (as in Rom. 8:15,23) but to birth, and in this there is a parallel with the Son. He is the one who was born of God (5:18 – *gennetheis*, the aorist tense denoting a specific event is used);[18] they are those who have been born of God (the same verb is used, but in the perfect tense). It is God who is 'begetter' (5:1); those who have been born of God are those who believe (5:1), but there is nothing to tie the moment of birth to conversion, to baptism or to some other moment.

Those who are born of God are corporately children of God; they are bound then to love those who share the same parentage (5:1–2). This means that love of 'the brethren' or of 'one another' in 1 John is chiefly if not exclusively love only of fellow members of the community (see below, pp. 68–9). That 'everyone who loves has been born of God' (4:7) does not mean that anyone anywhere who exercises love can be called a child of God, but that love is the defining characteristic of believers.

To be born of God is also to be possessed of a certain assurance. Birth cannot be reversed, neither does it happen by stages or in degrees! The one who has been born of God cannot, for that very reason, sin (3:9 – see below, pp. 61–2), 'because his seed (*sperma*) remains in him'. Grammatically this might be God's 'seed' or offspring who remain in God and so are kept from sin, or God's implanted seed which remains in the believer affording protection from sin. If the latter, is this 'implant' God's spirit, word or some other gift? This ambiguity invites comparison with our discussion of the 'chrisma' in 2:20,27 (above, pp. 28–30), and, as there, nothing in the context suggests a reference to the spirit unless we should suppose that in both cases the author prefers to use appropriate images for the spirit without naming it as such. As there too, it has been suggested that the image is one adopted from the author's (more gnostic?) opponents who claimed a special

---

[18] It seems best to see a reference to Jesus here, although this is the only place where 1 John uses the verb 'begotten' of Jesus, and the reference is denied by Brown, *Epistles*, 620–2, who favours a reference to the Christian with no distinction in the change of tense.

portion of the divine, but this explanation is not necessary. In 1 John 2:20,27 I suggested that 'the anointing' refers to the 'word' of God, which elsewhere is often represented by 'seed' (Mark 4:14); similarly in John 8:31–5 abiding in Jesus' word leads into being freed from sin.[19] Yet there is another equally probable source for the image: this whole passage, 1 John 3:7–17, reflects the story of Cain in Gen. 4, particularly as that story was developed in Jewish exegesis where Cain is the offspring of the devil, and where, being evil, he kills his righteous brother, Abel, after a dispute about the justice of God.[20] The 'seed' theme belongs to the Cain story already in the biblical text (Gen. 3:17; 4:25); since Eve greets Seth on his birth as 'another seed', it was natural for an interpretation to develop, found in both later Jewish and gnostic sources, that the seed from Adam (and in some interpreters the messianic seed) was carried not by Cain the first born but by Seth (and by those of his line). The point in 1 John 3:9 may be that God's seed is to be found not in Cain and his contemporary 'followers' but in those of God's choice, who have been born of him.

The absolute confidence that is thus given (see also 5:18), namely that it is of the very nature of those who have been born of God that they do not sin, is also expressed in the dualism which breathes through this passage. The alternatives are being born of God or being of the devil, being children of God or of the devil (3:8,10). Yet the alternative is not 'to be *born*' of the devil; this means that no answer is given to the questions how people become children of the devil and whether the devil plays an active role in this, as does God in begetting his children; it also raises the question whether this birth is simply a metaphor for dependence or does point to a communication of life and nature from God.

The visible sign of parentage is the presence or absence of

---

[19] In the light of other parallels between John 8 and 1 John 3 (see below, p. 40) it is interesting that *sperma* is used in the phrase 'seed of Abraham' in John 8:33,37, but this may be coincidental, for the meaning seems different.

[20] A number of commentators note the wider influence of the Cain narrative but without including the 'seed' theme: see Smalley, *1, 2, 3 John*, 183–8; N. Dahl, 'Der Erstgeborene Satans und der Vater des Teufels', in *Apophoreta. Festschrift für E. Haenchen* (Berlin, 1964), 70–84, 79–82.

brotherly love, the doing of righteousness or of sin (3:10); but not only are these the sign, they are also its inevitable (*cannot*) consequence. This means that 'being children of God' is not just likeness to or a relationship with God, although this is involved (2:29), but is to do with the very nature of the believer ('we are called children of God, and so we are', 3:1). Similarly, the consequent freedom from sin is not just freedom from committing certain acts but belonging to the sphere where sin has no place and where the evil one cannot touch the one born of God (5:18). So, inevitably, everything born of God – the whole totality (neuter) – conquers the world which stands in opposition to God (5:4).

Birth from God or to be a child of God has already been given; it is not a goal to be awaited or fully realised, for what is yet in store is 'to be like him' (3:2), perhaps implying the overcoming of the dependency of the child. Yet if being a child belongs to the incomplete present, this does not mean one can grow from childhood to maturity: the emphasis is on divine begetting and origin, not on immaturity.

This emphasis on the static quality of what the believer 'is', and its dualist setting, particularly in 3:7–10, begins to suggest two divinely intended groups fixed in an unchanging opposition which has been mysteriously generated by the polarity in the divine world between God and the devil. A rigid or mechanical dualism is avoided only because the defining characteristics of birth from God are acts of the will, loving the 'brother' or fellow child of God and believing. Yet it is what the letter does not say which prevents any sense of these choices as being predetermined. It is left unanswered whether there is an indeterminate middle ground out of which those who make a commitment to faith and love become children of God and those who actively reject such a commitment become children of the devil; or whether all are children of the devil until some become children of God; or, again, whether just as because they are children of God they cannot sin (3:9), so because they were *already* in some mysterious or implicit way children of God, they became believers.

These are dilemmas inherent in any dualist scheme and not

unique to 1 John; they are particularly sharply etched here because 1 John looks only to the present and does not reflect on any initial decision made by believers. Thus the Fourth Gospel, while sharing some of the same imagery, places the emphasis elsewhere. Only once in John are believers described as born of God (aorist – the perfect is used once of Jesus in 18:37, but apparently of his human birth and not a birth 'of God'); there, to be children of God is a gift for those who believe (John 1:12–13). In John 3 'birth' is from above or from (of) the spirit (and water) and is opposed to (natural) birth 'from the flesh';[21] the Gospel here does not use the imagery of children, nor is there any contrast with origin from the devil (but cf. 8:44). In John 3 it is also clear that this birth is an option laid before the individual which demands a response, while at the same time its generating power is not human but divine. It is the first element in this tension, the necessity for decision, which is less visible in 1 John. In the aftermath of schism and faced with having to set out clearly the essential character of the community of believers, it was the sharp contrast between being on one or other side of the divide which needed emphasising (see further below on the dualism of 1 John, pp. 80–7).

For a partial antecedent to 1 John's thought we can look again to the Old Testament, where Sonship belongs to the covenant relationship into which God brings his people (Exod. 4:22; Deut. 32:5f.; Wisd. 12:19f.). Yet this explains neither the dualist framework nor the concern with divine begetting in 1 John, which, as we have seen, lacks an explicit covenantal pattern.[22] Again the Qumran literature provides some parallels, particularly in the contrast between the sons of light and those of darkness, those born of truth and those of falsehood,

---

21 In this chapter there seems to be little difference between the perfect (6,8) and aorist (3,4,5,7) tenses. The imagery of birth from above or the spirit (in the Gospel) should not be identified directly with that of birth of God (in the Epistle). This contrast between Gospel and Epistles is only overcome when 'Johannine' theology of 'birth' from God is developed, as it is by M. Vellanickal, *The Divine Sonship of Christians in the Johannine Writings*, AnBib 72 (Rome, 1977), who explores the origins of this birth via the Gospel and the resulting life via the Epistle.

22 An alternative, not adopted here, would be to assume an implicit covenantal framework in 1 John; see above, pp. 32–3 and n. 16; Brown, *Epistles*, 389–90.

the children of righteousness and those of falsehood (1QS 3:19–4:26);[23] yet here too the covenant framework remains important and the specific image of divine begetting is not found.

Theologically, no doubt, the birth of believers from God must be dependent on the birth of Jesus from God; so is this how the thought of 1 John has developed? Psalm 2:7, 'Thou art my Son, this day I have begotten thee', is of christological significance throughout the New Testament (see Acts 13:33) and could be seen as the model for the begetting of believers. However, this Psalm has little significance in the Johannine corpus, and 1 John makes little of the priority of Jesus as the one who was begotten (see above, pp. 33–4). Others have pointed to a baptismal origin for the image of begetting, supposing that that is the background for its use in 1 Pet. 1:3,23; Titus 3:5; but the setting in 1 John is not obviously baptismal, nor would this account for the contrast with being children of the devil.[24]

The importance of the image of divine begetting in 1 John has led some to look for a background in Hellenistic thought, and particularly in mystery religions or gnosticism. However, most of the sources for these are of a later date, and the underlying presuppositions are different: rebirth there is an experience of the soul or a rediscovery of its true nature.[25] Yet, read on its own outside the framework provided by the rest of the New Testament or the Old Testament, the language of 1 John would probably sound familiar to Hellenistic readers, not least with its sharp dualism and self-confident assurance over against the world.

---

23 The relationship of this passage to the Johannine tradition is explored by J. H. Charlesworth, 'A Critical Comparison of the Dualism in 1QS 3:13–4:26 and the "Dualism" Contained in the Gospel of John', in *John and Qumran*, ed. J. H. Charlesworth (London, 1972), 76–106, although his conclusion (104) that 'John probably borrowed some of his dualistic terminology and mythology from 1QS 3:13–4:26' goes beyond the evidence of the parallels.

24 See above, pp. 7–8 and n. 12 on the theory of W. Nauck. Schnackenburg, *Johannesbriefe*, 192–3 does argue that the image is baptismal in 1 John and that 'children of the devil' is formed in analogy, but refers only to a moral belonging, so offering only an apparent parallel with 'children of God'.

25 See Schnackenburg, *Johannesbriefe*, 180–2; F. Büchsel, 'gennao', *TDNT* 1, 665–75, 671.

Of God

Not only are believers born of God or children of God; they are simply 'of God' (*ek theou*; the images are used closely together in 3:10 and 5:18–19). Clearly more than belonging to or coming from God is meant; the phrase points to a divine origin. It too is used as a firm affirmation – *You* or *We* are of God (4:4,6; 5:19) – which offers further assurance; it is the source of the victory over the opponents already won (4:4), of the assured freedom from sin and the evil one (5:19). The alternative is not simply 'not [yet] being of God'; it is being of the world – having the world as the origin of one's existence (4:5). This does not mean mere natural existence, for the world is under the evil one (5:9; see also 2:16). More explicitly in chapter 3, under the influence of the story of Cain, not to be of God is to be of the devil or of the evil one (3:8,12). There are spirits which are of God and those which are not; the latter are of 'error' or even of 'the antichrist' (4:2–3,6). The parallelism suggests a real symmetry between being of God or of the devil (but see n. 24), although never are those 'of the devil' said to have been 'born of the devil'.

To be of God is to be characterised by doing righteousness, not by doing sin, presumably by loving (since love is 'of God', 4:7), and by living in the confidence already described. Yet there is an ambiguity about the identity of those 'of God'. In 4:6 those who know God and who, by implication, are 'of God' hear and respond to 'us'. Are these existing members of the community who have yet to openly take sides? Outwardly undifferentiated, it has yet to be demonstrated whether they are truly 'of us' (2:29); support of 'us' will demonstrate the authenticity of the apparent knowledge of God and being of God of those still uncommitted. Or are those 'of God' in 4:6 outsiders? In 4:5 the author speaks of the erstwhile members of the community as 'of the world, speaking of the world and listened to by the world' (and not by 'those of the world'); apparently they are engaged in a mission to non-believers, a largely successful mission. This could mean that in 4:6 'we' too are engaged in such a mission, largely unsuccessful but occasionally winning a response from those who are (unconsciously

or potentially) 'of God'. If so, the division between those who
are of God and those who are of the world is to be found not just
in the community but in all humanity, or at least all who come
into contact with the community; there is no prior neutrality.

This is a problem we have already met (pp. 36–7), and to
which 1 John does not supply the answer. There may always be
the tendency for any dualism, even one which originates in a
conflict between two circumscribed groups, to move towards a
division which cuts through all humankind as well as through
the 'heavenly' or supra-human sphere (God versus the devil;
the spirit of truth versus the spirit of error). However, the main
motivating point for 1 John does not lie in a theory of the
universe or of God or of the material world, but in the sense of
being a beleaguered minority needing affirmation; hence the
negative side of the dualism is less developed than the positive
and there is limited interest in the supra-natural dimension.

No doubt the idea of being 'of God' has come to 1 John from
earlier tradition. The formula is found only in the Johannine
writings in the New Testament. In John 8 it is Jesus' opponents
who do not listen to his word (which is God's word) and so
prove themselves to be not 'of God' but of their father the devil
(John 8:44,47 – a passage also influenced by the story of Cain);
there is no explicit contrast with being 'of the world' in this
chapter, although it may be implicit elsewhere (8:23; 15:19;
17:14,16). In 3 John 11, in an antithesis which has the same
form as many in 1 John, 'the one who does good is of God, the
one who does evil has not seen God'.[26] In both these cases the
image is independent of those of birth or of being children of
God; indeed the Gospel uses the '(being) of' formula with a
variety of other terms – being from (of) below or above, from
the earth or heaven, from this world or not of this world (8:23;
3:31; 15:19; 17:14–16; 18:36; 6:32). In 1 John the formula is
much more narrow, and he uses only 'of the truth' (1 John 3:19;
2:19; cf. John 18:37), and 'of the world', which is contrasted not
with 'not of the world' but with 'of God'. Although sharing a
common heritage, the formula therefore has a different 'feel' in

[26] Houlden, *Epistles*, 154 suggests that this verse may be part of the same series of
aphorisms which provided the antithetical statements of 1 John.

John from in 1 John; in the Gospel it suggests belonging and quality or perhaps source, while in the Epistle its association with birth and its limited use with other terms suggest both causal origin and essence.

It looks as if two factors have led to 1 John's use of 'of God'. It has been assimilated to the language of 'birth from God', giving it a less general or flexible meaning, and, perhaps as a result of the schism within the community, it has been brought into a developing dualist scheme whose potential consequences have not been fully worked through. There is something of a tension between the apparent universal reference of the language (world, devil) and the author of 1 John's concern with those who have left the community and need to secure the defences against further losses. The relationship between the theological framework within which 1 John works and the circumstances and experience of its readers is an important issue for exploring its continuing significance.

Abiding and having

'Abiding' (*menein*) is a characteristic Johannine term for the relationship between the believer and God or Jesus, although the Gospel's use is not identical with that of 1 John.[27] In 1 John abiding is a fully reciprocal experience – believers, or those who obey God's commands and live in love, abide in God as God does in them (3:24; 4:12–16); in the same way abiding in death is identical with not having life abiding in one (3:14–15). In contrast to the Gospel (John 6:56; 15:1–7), abiding is predominantly theocentric – in and by God – although the frequent and characteristic 'in him' does allow for some ambiguity as to whether God or Jesus is intended (2:6,28; 3:6,24; 4:13), and in 2:24 abiding is 'in the Son and in the Father'.

Abiding is a claim the believer can justifiably make, but only when that claim is matched by a life of obedience and love (2:5–6; see below on 'being in him'); such obedience both is a precondition and at times seems almost a definition of abiding

---

[27] On abiding see J. Heise, *BLEIBEN: Menein in den johanneischen Schriften* (Tübingen, 1967); Malatesta, *Interiority and Covenant*.

in and by God (3:24; 4:12,16). Although the image could be a universal one, it remains true only of members of the community of believers: 'If we love one another, God abides in us' (4:12) is addressed to believers and not to humankind; as we have seen, love of one another is restricted to the community.

Abiding can be a source of assurance as much as can birth from or being of God – 'Everyone who abides in him does not sin' (3:6) – but unlike the other formulae it can also be urged upon them: 'Abide in him!' (2:27–8). It would be hard to urge someone to be born! So also, abiding can be tested and evidenced in more 'visible' ways – by the spirit (3:24; 4:13). However, it is not clear what form this evidence would take; the spirit is not simply identified with God or Jesus 'in us', but neither does 1 John suggest any particular 'spirit-activity'.

The exhortation to abide is not an exhortation to endurance and perseverance (as at Mark 14:34); it is a continuing relationship which does not envisage change or development (2:17, 'abides for ever'). They do abide, they must abide. The reverse is not expressed except as abiding in death (3:14–15); at 2:9–10 the reverse of abiding in the light is *being still* in the darkness, but the change of verb may not be significant. Not only God abides in believers: the word of God abides in the young men (2:14), God's seed abides in the one born of God, offering protection from sin (3:9), while 'his anointing' abides in members of the community, relieving them of any need of a teacher (2:27). So too they are to be sure that what they have heard from the beginning abides in them (2:24), and if it does they will abide not in it but in the Son and the Father. Similarly 2:27 ends and the next verse starts with the same words '[you] abide in him', but in the former case 'him' is probably the anointing, or possibly its source (Jesus or God), while in 28 the reference is the one who will appear (again either Jesus or God; see below, p. 73). This fluidity and variation suggest that there is no great difference in experience between abiding when applied to 'things' and when applied to God. It also creates a bridge between the Johannine intimate relationship with God and the call to remain faithful to what has been received which has other NT parallels (Acts 14:22, 1 Tim. 2:15).

Perhaps identical with 'abiding' is 'being' (*einai*) in God (the two are parallel in 2:5–6), although the latter is less common (2:5; 5:20; ?4:4) and is not used in a reciprocal formula. Other subjects can also 'be in': truth, his word, love (which may also be perfected, 4:12) are 'in us' (1:8,10; 2:4); 'stumbling' or 'an offence' (*skandalon*) 'is not in' the one who loves a brother. The one who does not so love cannot rightly claim 'to be in the light' but 'is in the darkness' (2:9,11), for God is light and there is no darkness 'in him' (1:5).

There is more here than a place or sphere which is 'inhabited', but neither does the letter imply a mystical indwelling or union which annuls the separate identity of God or of the believer. Is abiding in or by God simply a metaphor for a moral identity of purpose? Does the reciprocal use of 'what you have heard', abiding 'in you' and 'you abiding in the Son and the Father' mean that the latter is just another way of saying the former, a manner of life and of faithfulness to the tradition? The very flexibility of the theme and the range of terms with which it can be used mean we cannot give a simple answer; the moral life, faithfulness to the tradition and to fellow members of the community, and the religious experience of community with God belong inseparably together, but it does not seem that they are to be simply equated with each other.

For this reason 'abiding' is both an individual experience (3:6, 4:15,16b) and a corporate one. That 'we abide in him and he in us' (4:13) refers just as naturally to God's presence in the community, so that the evidence of the spirit is a community rather than an individual experience; so also in 2:24,27–8 it is the community who are to keep hold of the message from the beginning and so are to enjoy that reciprocal fellowship with the Son and the Father (see also 1:3). There is a continual movement between the experience of the individual and that of the community: the one who keeps his commands abides in him (God?) and God in that person, and *we* know he abides in (?among) us by the spirit which he has given us (3:24).

All this is equally true of 'having' (*echein*) the Father or the Son (2:23; 5:12; 2 John 9). The phrase has been seen as a uniquely Johannine expression of personal fellowship, coined perhaps in opposition to 'gnostic' claims to possess God;[28] however, it may express little more than 'to hold on to': the one who denies the Son 'does not have the Father *either*', while the one who confesses the Son '*also* has the Father' (2:23; thus 'having' is virtually synonymous with believing – see also the parallel between 'believing in' and 'having' the Son in 5:10,12).[29] Yet 'to have' the Son is 'to have' life (5:12–13), which suggests a different nuance – it is impossible to strait-jacket 1 John's thought, and the various terms cannot be assimilated to each other.

In this way 1 John's use of 'abiding' or 'being' in, and of 'having' is more flexible than that of 'birth' or even 'know-ledge' of God. It is not kept within a dualistic framework; it can be used both for assurance and for exhortation, while the range of terms or images with which it is combined gives clearest expression to the fundamental theme of the letter that the authenticity of any relationship with God is rooted in and inseparable from their manner of life in faithfulness to the tradition, to the commands and to one another.

The roots of 1 John's thought are not easy to trace. Certainly the *idea* of divine immanence can be found elsewhere, but not the particular use of the verb 'to abide' (*menein*).[30] The Old Testament knows the quest for God's dwelling with his people both in the cult (Psalm 46:5) and in eschatological hope (Joel 2:27), and that is a hope which can be centred on the individual (Jer. 31:31f.?). Yet this tradition does not prepare us for the distinctive reciprocity of the Johannine formula. A similar reciprocity is found in the Gospel in the mutual 'abiding' of Jesus and the believer (John 6:56; 15:5f.); more frequently expressed without the verb 'to abide', this new Jesus-centred experience or status is grounded in the mutual 'in-being' of Father and Son (10:38; 14:10–11,20; 17:21,23,26). This

---

[28] H. Hanse, 'echein', *TDNT* II, 816–27, 823–4.

[29] A similar use comes in *T. Dan.* 5:2, 'and be at peace, holding to the God of peace'. This meaning may not fit 2 John 9 so well (where, unlike 1 John, the phrase 'does not have *God*' is also used), but it does seem that this verse is modelled on or related to those of 1 John.

[30] See Brown, *Epistles*, 261, 283–4; Malatesta, *Interiority and Covenant*, 42–77, esp. 58–64.

dynamic is not shared by 1 John, which says nothing about the inner divine relationship and looks at 'abiding' as a God-centred reality. Perhaps all we can say is that from a common and distinctive heritage the two writings have used the 'immanence' theme in their own way, and that in 1 John it expresses at once religious confidence and the need to maintain faithfulness in the community and to its tradition.[31]

The spirit

The spirit must surely belong to the religious experience of the believer (s), although it is also seen as something outward and recognisable which can confirm the validity of claims to inner experience; that 'we have known him' can be tested by 'keeping his commands', that 'he abides in us' 'by the spirit he has given us' (2:3; 3:24). The spirit is not a key theme, and little is said about it. He (God?) has given us his spirit, or perhaps (a portion) of his spirit; the act of giving need not be tied to a specific occasion such as baptism, for it is expressed in the less particular perfect tense (4:13) as well as in the aorist (3:24). The assertion, twice repeated, that the gift of the spirit is proof of divine indwelling brackets a strong word of caution: 'Beloved, believe not every spirit!' (4:1). That 'visible' proof is after all open to false identification. Some may be possessors of a spirit which is not that given by God, the spirit of error and not of truth (4:6), indeed that which stems from the antichrist (see below).

The mark of the true as of the false spirit lies in their confession of Jesus, or rather in that made by their bearers (4:2–3; see below); the significance of the false confession is not immediately clear, but presumably it represents neither total unbelief nor self-evident perversity, otherwise testing would not be necessary. Although much ink has been spilt on attempting to identify the false belief, this is not the author's concern – he speaks only of *not* confessing Jesus (or 'dissolving',

---

[31] Again this distinction is overcome when a harmonising 'Johannine' theology is developed; so Vellanickal, *Divine Sonship*, 308, 315; A. Feuillet, *Le Mystère de l'amour divin dans la théologie Johannique*, EBib (Paris, 1972), 194, who thus sees the Gospel and Epistle as complementary and inseparable.

perhaps denying the power of, Jesus).[32] His chief concern is to affirm the community in their real victory and to underline the critical nature of the present conflict.

From this passage it would seem that there is more than one spirit, but perhaps only two, the spirit of God or of truth and the spirit of error. God has given of his spirit; others presumably have received the spirit of error (perhaps from the antichrist, but this is far from explicit). There are here strong linguistic parallels with the Dead Sea Scrolls, which also speak of the two spirits, of truth and of falsehood, in which humankind walks, and with the *Testaments of the Twelve Patriarchs*.[33] Yet the parallels are mainly of language and not of essential conception. Unlike the Jewish sources, in 1 John the two spirits are not dispositions or tendencies already inherent in individuals; nor are they possibilities of allegiance or action before which the believer must make his or her choice. They are ascribed no cosmic dimension and do not represent heavenly forces locked in combat, and they are not part of the divine purpose.[34]

The letter itself suggests that the confidence given or expressed in the gift of the spirit has been shaken. A solution to this has been found by an appeal to an eschatological tradition which does not match the mood of the Epistle as a whole. The caution against false prophets as a means to interpret the crisis, like the warning about the antichrist, is in formulaic language which belongs to an eschatological tradition with echoes elsewhere in the NT (Matt. 24:11; Rev. 19:20). Therefore we cannot assume from this language that the spirit was experienced in a prophetic or 'charismatic' way in the community of 1 John, or that prophetic or charismatic enthusiasm lay at the heart of the schism; neither is there anything to support the

---

[32] That the spirit not of God 'looses' (*luei*) Jesus is a less well-attested reading but may be preferred because it is the more difficult to explain; see Brown, *Epistles*, 494–6, and below, pp. 75–6.

[33] Especially 1QS 3:13–4:26: 'He has created man to govern the world, and has appointed for him two spirits in which to walk until the time of His visitation: the spirits of truth and falsehood' (1QS 3:18; see n. 23 above); *T. Sim.* 3.1, 'Beware the Spirit of deceit and envy'; *T. Reub.* 2:1; 3:2,7 speaks of seven spirits of deceit etc.

[34] 1QS 4:16–17: 'For God has established the spirits in equal measure until the final age, and has set everlasting hatred between their divisions.'

idea that the author's opponents manifested or claimed particular gifts. Indeed, I John itself nowhere indicates that the spirit's activity might be differentiated into a variety of gifts. There is no parallel with the call to 'distinguish' between spirits in I Cor. 12:10. The only mark of the spirit and the only concern of the author is true confession.[35]

The spirit not of God is the spirit of error (4:6) – the spirit is the source of error or (perhaps and) originates in error. Error and deception are also 'eschatological' themes – they represent the ultimate threat in the final conflict even for believers (Mark 13:22; 2 Thess. 2:8–12), a threat I John well knows (2:26; 3:7). The opponent of such a spirit, originating in reality from God, is necessarily the spirit of truth. The language in its dualistic framework is closer to that of the intertestamental sources cited earlier than to the Fourth Gospel's use of the same phrase 'spirit of truth' (14:7; 15:26; 16:13), even though it is peculiar to these two writings within the New Testament.[36]

The spirit is experienced within the community, for it is there that confession is made and tested. 'The spirit [which] he gave to us' (4:13) points to a corporate experience; in 4:4, 'the one who is in you is greater than the one who is in the world' again contrasts the community with the world – the reference is perhaps to the spirit, although it might be to God or to Christ. The focus is on the spirit present in the community rather than in the hearts of individual believers, and it is the community rather than the individual which provides the battlefield.[37] This means we should not think of the spirits as the spirits of particular individuals under inspiration by the divine or by the antichrist. Although the spirit is described as God's spirit (4:13) as well as as God's gift, it is not related to the divine life any more explicitly, and the parallel with 'the spirit of error' or 'that of the antichrist' cautions against forcing

---

[35] Schnackenburg, 'Die johanneischen Gemeinde und ihre Geisterfahrung', in *Die Kirche des Anfangs*, 277–306, suggests that the Johannine community may not have known prophecy and that the spirit was particularly, but not exclusively, associated with preaching and teaching.

[36] The Gospel does not use 'spirit of truth' in a dualist setting and knows no opposing spirit; instead the spirit of truth communicates the divine revelation which is the truth.

[37] Against Malatesta, *Interiority and Covenant*, 282, who sees it as individual.

any deeper relationship, such as looking for its mediation by Jesus.

Even if the spirit were represented by 'the anointing' (2:20,27) or the 'seed' (3:7), the very ambiguity of these images does little to suggest any richer understanding, although the emphasis on teaching rather than on any more 'prophetic' activity might be confirmed. Otherwise the spirit appears only in the complex passage, 5:6–8. Here again the spirit combines with (is!) the truth, and the context is essentially confessional: the spirit is the one which bears witness. Joined with that witness is the witness of the water and the blood; as a unity their witness is either identical with, or leads to, the witness which God himself has borne to his Son (7–9).

The precise nature of the spirit in this passage is as obscure as that of the water and of the blood to which, as the means of Jesus' coming (6c), and with which (8) the spirit witnesses. Some have seen the spirit as inspired utterance testifying to the necessity of Jesus' death (blood) for the release of spiritual blessing (water). Others, recognising an echo of John 19:34, point to the spirit-inspiration of the Beloved Disciple whose witness, there affirmed, to the water and blood from the side of Jesus continued in the testimony of the 'we' of the Johannine school; in this case a continuity with the Gospel is seen in the association of the spirit with the witness of John the Baptist (John 1:32) and of the disciples (15:26–7).[38] Others, seeing in the witness of the water and the blood a sacramental reference, argue for the spirit here witnessing through them. For others again the witness of the spirit is through the inner experience of faith.[39] We must hope that the section had a more immediate meaning for its first than for its modern readers.

It seems probable that these verses, like the related but not necessarily formative John 19:34, reflect themes important for the Johannine community. Although the spirit alone is called

---

[38] Grayston, *Epistles*, 138, speaks of the 'inspired utterance' claimed by the 'we' group of 1:1–4 in faithfulness to the tradition; Smalley, *1, 2, 3 John*, 282, stresses the continuity with the witness given in the ministry of Jesus.

[39] A sacramenal reference is found by Schnackenburg, *Johannesbriefe*, 261–3, while G. Schunack, *Die Briefe des Johannes* (Zurich, 1982), 95, talks of the spirit within the 'testimony of faith', with a cross-reference to the 'anointing' in 2:20,27.

the truth, in v. 8 it is grammatically put on an equal footing with the water and the blood, albeit in first place, and cannot necessarily be said to have priority over or to work through them. In v. 9 human witness and the witness of God are contrasted, but in terms of the argument the witness of the spirit could be identified with either of these – and since in the following verses (9b–11) only the witness given by God is mentioned, we may suspect that the witness of spirit, water and blood is the 'lesser' human (of men) witness.[40]

The experience of the spirit, while an aspect of religious experience for 1 John, does not stand at its centre and is only cautiously articulated. This is not because the opposition have 'hijacked' the theme, preventing the author from adopting it, for any polemical interpretation of the letter has to assume that the author is well able to cite, remould and forge into weapons his opponents' rallying cries. That the spirit poses something of a problem is true, but even if this were not so, it is likely that the author would not present a more sophisticated understanding of the spirit's work.[41]

THE TESTS OF LIFE

In the last section we have isolated and analysed the various expressions of the relationship with God. This is something 1 John does not do. Although different terms predominate in different settings, 'born of God' not appearing before 2:29 and 'children of God' coming only in chapter 3 and 5:2, they are often used in parallel or in similar contexts, implying variety but not sharp distinction or development.[42] Again, we have explored these themes on their own, but the major concern of the letter is that they are never independent of lives lived.

[40] If the 'this is' points backwards, then the testimony of God would be that of the spirit, water and blood, but more probably it points forward to what follows.
[41] This is in contrast to J. Coetzee, 'The Holy Spirit in 1 John', *Neotestamentica* 13 (1981), 43–66 who sees 5:6–12 (and hence the teaching of the spirit) as holding a key position in 1 John.
[42] Contrast B. F. Westcott, *The Epistles of St. John* (London, 1883), 119–21 who sees 'birth from God' as expressing the initial communication of divine life, 'being of God' as the resultant essential connection, and 'child of God' as that which the believer thus becomes.

When contradicted by clear 'tests of life' all such claims to religious experience are but self-deception. It is not just 'You' or 'We' 'are born of God!' but 'the one born of God *does* or *does not* ... '. Testing and assurance are held in balance, and having explored the assurance we must now turn to the testing. Despite this, for the readers of the letter the balance is tipped on the side of assurance – they indeed have conquered ... (2:14–16; 4:4f.).

Testing and debate

Not only is testing directly urged – 'Do not believe every spirit but test the spirits' (4:1) – but the structure of the letter itself reproduces the process of self-analysis and testing. The opening section is built around a debate about what 'we', the community, may rightly say: 'If we say we have fellowship with him and walk in darkness we deceive ourselves' (1:6). This is not aimed at others who did so claim but at the community, 'we', who must test their own claims, for this was a claim they could and did make – 'that you also may have fellowship with us and our fellowship is with the Father ... ' (1:3). '*By this* we know that we have known him, *if* we keep his commandments' (2:3); the certainty that they have known him (2:13) can and must be so verified. The debate explores both the negative – when a claim may be self-deception – and the positive, where 'we' no longer merely 'say' but actually do walk in the light and confess sins (1:7,9). Indeed 'to say' always implies a negative, the invalidity of the claim (1:6,8,10; cf. 2:4,6,9; 4:20).

The debate also continues more impersonally about 'he who says' and 'does' (2:4,6,9–11; 3:7,8,14; 4:8) or 'everyone who ... ' (2:23; 3:4,6,9,10,15; 4:7; see also 'whoever ... ': 2:5; 3:17; 4:15; and 'if anyone ... ': 4:20; 5:16). Yet the apparently impersonal form does not mean that the community are not equally involved in this debate. As the continuity between 'we' and 'he who' in 2:3–4 shows, it is the same group, the community, who are in mind. The patterns of religious experience and behaviour being explored here are again those characteristic of the community: claiming to have known him (2:4), to be in the light (2:9, cf. 1:7), to abide in him or be born of him (3:6,9) and, most importantly, to believe and to love (2:10; 3:14; 4:7,20; 5:1,10).[43]

It is often argued that the negative examples, claims falsified by the tests of behaviour, refer directly to the author's opponents, the schismatics; the failings thus implied and the claims have then been used to draw a profile of these opponents and to identify them with known movements in the early church.[44] This, however, is to ignore the urgency of the debate for the author himself. There are indeed hints that the schismatics, who are only defined in terms of their failures in confession (2:18–27; 4:1–6), may have prompted the moral debate – the two topics are linked by the theme of lying and of deception (2:21, cf. 1:6; 2:4; 2:26, cf. 3:7; 1:8). Yet these hints are not developed and the debate about tests, the so-called 'moral debate', is conducted without reference to the 'antichrist (s)'. Whatever the erstwhile members of the community had said or done, the issue is a living internal one for the community, at least as the author perceives it. In the debate we do not see ruthless attack against some external opposition but a genuine wrestling with the implications of religious experience, particularly when that experience is expressed as a 'realised' present reality.

The tests of life[45]

The importance of this testing and debate in the letter gives the impression that a major concern is the ethical consequences of Christian experience; the harvest of such consequences is surprisingly meagre.[46]

---

[43] See J. M. Lieu, 'Authority to Become Children of God: A Study of 1 John', *NovT* 23 (1981), 210–28, 221–4.

[44] See above, pp. 13–15.

[45] This is the title given a study of 1 John by R. Law, *The Tests of Life* (Edinburgh, 1909).

[46] See J. L. Houlden, *Ethics and the New Testament* (Harmondsworth, 1973), 38–40.

The tests which may falsify or validate religious experience can be briefly listed:

Walking in the darkness *vs.* walking in the light (as he is in the light)	1:6
(ought to walk as he walked)	2:6
(Not) keeping his commands or his word	2:3–6; 3:24; 5:2
Hating *vs.* loving one's brother (Here being or walking in the light or darkness has become the religious claim or experience)	2:9–11; 3:14–15; 4:7–8,20; ?5:2 (cf. 4:16)
Doing sin or sinning *vs.* not sinning or doing righteousness (as he is righteous) = loving a brother	3:4,7–10
(By the spirit he has given us	3:24; 4:13)

What is the content of these behavioural norms? That they are 'his' commands points to their origin with God (3:22–4; 5:2–3) rather than with Jesus (although 2:3–4 and 4:21 are ambiguous). Although the demand to keep the commands features more than their content,[47] the variation between the plural and the singular (as in 3:22–4) excludes any idea of a developed pattern of rules and instead focusses on the one command. This is ultimately the command to love (3:11; 4:21) or, distinctively, 'that we believe in the name of his son Jesus Christ and love one another' (3:23). Even the apparently more general 'we do what is pleasing before him' (3:22) appears in the following verses to refer no more widely than to mutual love.

Sinning, doing sin or doing righteousness take us little further. Sin is a problem for the letter, apparently both possible for 'a brother' (5:16; cf. 1:9f.) and yet incompatible with 'abiding in him' (3:6), a problem to which we shall return. Yet what is sin? According to 3:4 it is lawlessness (*anomia*); although this is a general OT word for sin, it can also designate the ultimate iniquity in opposition to God's rule which would be characteristic of the End-time. In the context of chapter 3 this meaning fits better than simply contravention of the Law

---

[47] The content of the command is expressed only in 3:23 and 4:21 (and 3:11 as 'the message'), the necessity and consequences of keeping them in 2:3–4,7–8; 3:22,24; 5:2–3.

or of the rules of the community.[48] While this would explain why the believer cannot sin (namely cannot participate in such final opposition), it does not help define sin elsewhere in the letter. In the Gospel of John 'sin' is primarily unbelief or the refusal to believe, but this does not fit 1 John so well, where Christ was manifested to take away sins, and it is possible to say there is no sin in him (3:5) (see below, p. 75). In 3:10 'not doing righteousness' is expanded as 'not loving one's brother' and in the following verses this is developed with reference to the story of Cain's hatred and murder of his brother Abel (3:12,15). That story of the first murder is probably already in mind in 3:8, where the devil is described as 'sinning from the beginning'. This could suggest that for 1 John sin is ultimately the failure to love; this has been particularly manifested in the life of the community, but it can be set on a wider stage of archetypal hatred. Even if this is too precise and the author assumed that all would know what sinning entailed, there is nothing to suggest that sin is a matter of relationships outside the community or of the contravention of any other received moral norms.

'Walking in the light' or 'in the darkness' may equally be so self-evident as to need no exposition. Yet in 2:9f. being or walking in the light rather than in the darkness is no longer that by which claims to religious experience may be tested, but is itself such a claim or inner reality which may be tested by the more visible loving or hating a brother. Walking in the light is not simply a matter of right behaviour but is a sphere of existence – light, as God is in the light (1:6), or darkness, which is opposed to the light and which, like the world, is passing away (2:8,17). We are left with the sense that for 1 John it is the internal relationships within the community, love for one another, which are the ultimate visible manifestation of the sphere in which people move. Only once does such love take clearer form – in practical response to the brother, the fellow believer, who is in need (3:17). That is to love in active truth and not in word alone.

One passage, not part of the tests of life, may suggest that the

[48] As proposed by Houlden, *Epistles*, 92.

moral life of believers should extend beyond love for one another. The world is not to be loved, because everything which belongs to the world (literally 'in the world') is not of God, 'the desire of the flesh, the desire of the eyes and the pride of life' (2:16). This can be read in a 'Johannine' framework – 'the flesh' is that which is not the spirit, the eyes represent the sight which does not see with faith (contrast 1:1), and life (*bios*) is natural and not eternal (*zoe*) life – 'all three describe a world into which the light of God's son has not yet penetrated'.[49] In this case the verse only characterises the life of 'the world', life outside the life of faith and of the community. Attractive as this reading is, it pays insufficient attention to the use of 'desire' and 'pride', while 'flesh' is not opposed to spirit in this Epistle – it otherwise occurs only at 4:2 – and in its remaining use 'life' means wealth (3:17). 'Desire', although in itself neutral, is often used in a negative sense in the Old Testament (Num. 11:4; Ps. 106:14) and also in the New of the way of life Christians (should) have left behind (Gal. 5:16; Eph. 2:3). It seems most probable that our passage belongs to this tradition, although the threefold pattern suggests it has become a stock formula characterising the world. It would then be wrong to try to identify the 'vices' more specifically – such as whether 'the desire of the eyes' is sexual lust or covetousness or (against a more Greek background) being captivated by the material world – or to suggest that 1 John is advocating an ascetic life-style rejecting every type of sensuality.[50]

Experience and obedience

If we may speak in this restricted sense of the 'ethics' of 1 John, the author sees the believer's life in relation with God as the *source* of ethical behaviour. What is its basis – what motivates and determines the particular pattern 1 John advocates? Like

---

[49] Brown, *Epistles*, 312.
[50] This interpretation follows N. Lazure, *Les Valeurs morales de la théologie Johannique* (Paris, 1965), 320–6; Lazure prefers a Hebraic background to a Greek one and sees 'the desire of the flesh' as a more general statement encompassing the other two, sexual lust and the over-valuing of wealth.

most of the NT writings, 1 John offers a number of answers, which are not fully integrated with each other.[51]

Overriding in importance is obedience to 'his' commands, ultimately *the* command to love one another. The ambiguity as to whether 'his' refers to God or to Jesus shows that there is no particular appeal to 'a word from the Lord'; this is even true in the words 'as he gave us a command' (3:23), where, although the aorist tense of the verb points to a specific moment such as in the ministry of Jesus, the context points to a reference to God. The command can also be termed 'his word' (2:5), which looks back to the 'word of life' of the prologue (1:1). It also invites obedience because it is no new imposition; it belongs to that which goes back to 'the beginning', to the foundation of the community or of its members' faith (2:7; see above, pp. 30–1). As such it is part of their identity and to be faithful to the command is to be faithful to the community's identity; to fail to obey the command would be a denial of and destructive of the community's existence.[52]

At the same time the command is new – because it belongs to the same sphere as do believers, to the sphere of God and of the light rather than to that of the world and of darkness, to the sphere of the future, which is already coming in the present, rather than to that of the present, which is already becoming past (2:8,17). All this reflects a dualism and also an eschatology which will need further exploration (see below, pp. 80–7). Thus to hate is to belong to the sphere of darkness and of death or of the evil one (3:8); hatred is also characteristic of the world (3:13). As lawlessness sin is the eschatological opposition to God (see above, p. 52). Darkness and the world are passing away, the evil one has been conquered (2:13f.) and death has been left behind for those who have eternal life (3:14). To love is to belong to the sphere of light to which God himself belongs, and indeed is (1:7). Loving behaviour thus belongs to the side of God against that of the evil one and to the side of the new against that of the old.

Eschatology gives a further impetus to 'ethical' behaviour in view of 'his' coming or of the day of judgement, although these

[51] See Houlden, *Ethics*, 7–24.   [52] See Lieu, *Second and Third Epistles*, 73–6.

are equally, if not more so, a source of assurance. Boldness on the day of judgement (4:17) is given to those who are fully absorbed by love, for love and fear have no part in each other. Confidence in the face of 'his' (see below) coming results from remaining in him or doing righteousness even as he is righteous (2:28–9). In this eschatological context imitation (see below) has added force, and is inspired by the hope of the not-yet-revealed future ('We shall see him as he is', 3:2). However, unlike in some New Testament writers, the eschatological possibility of being judged and found wanting is not a motive for moral action in 1 John (contrast 1 Cor. 9:27; 2 Cor. 5:10).[53]

Imitation is not restricted to eschatological contexts. In 3:3,5,7, 'he' or 'that one' (*ekeinos*) probably refers to Jesus – he is pure, not possessing sin, righteous, and as such is a pattern to be followed. This use of the demonstrative pronoun 'that one', found also at 2:6; 3:16; 4:17, may reflect a pattern of catachesis. The one who claims to remain in 'him' should walk as 'that one' walked (2:6) – the past tense perhaps pointing to traditions about Jesus' earthly life, not necessarily only those we know from the Fourth Gospel. Elsewhere the present tense (he *is* righteous) is used, putting the emphasis on Jesus' present significance. These epithets are taken for granted as needing no description or justification; the only specific example is 'that one laid down his life for us; and we ought to lay down our lives for the brethren' (3:16; perhaps drawing on Johannine tradition: cf. John 15:13). However, a negative example for imitation can also be given which is not taken from the Jesus tradition – that of Cain (3:12).

Conformity with the nature of, if not imitation of, God is a further basis for behaviour: God is light (1:7) and love (4:7,16), and whatever the metaphysical meaning of such assertions, their goal is moral – fellowship with such a God means walking in the light, practising love. 'If you know that he is righteous, know that so also everyone who does righteousness has been born of him' (2:29) may be an appeal to the necessary likeness between begetter and begotten. Although the continuity from 2:28 is unclear, the final 'him' ('born of him') must be God,

[53] 3:19–20 probably offers reassurance rather than caution: see below, pp. 89–90.

which suggests that it is also God who is righteous (as perhaps at 1:9, although at 3:7; 2:1 this epithet belongs to Jesus) (see below, pp. 74–5).

A further ground for ethical behaviour elsewhere in the New Testament is often a devaluation of the (material) world.[54] For 1 John this means shunning the attractions or values of the world, of society apart from God and outside the community (2:15–17), although they are still to be used for the communal good (3:17: 'life', *bios*, is only used in these verses in the Johannine corpus). Elsewhere in the NT such a devaluation can accompany a real concern for the issues provoked by living in that society and for witnessing to it (as in Paul and 1 Peter), but 1 John does not exhibit such a concern, being focussed only on intra-communal relations. The one exception to this may be the closing verse of the letter, 'Keep yourselves from idols' (5:21). Taken literally this looks out on the worship of the pagan world at its most typical and most to be shunned, at least from a Jewish perspective (Acts 15:29; 1 Cor. 10:14; 1 Thess. 1:9). Yet nothing in the letter prepares us for a concern with the temptation to revert to paganism. It may be that the term is used metaphorically, just as the Qumran literature speaks of an apostate as one who 'walks among the idols of his heart' (1QS 2:11). We would expect something clearer from a final rallying exhortation, but perhaps it was clearer for the first readers, who were used to the author's metaphors and symbols![55]

In Christian thought there is often a tension between a stress on the priority of God's saving action and a call to human ethical striving;[56] in 1 John this is hardly visible except in the dilemma over the claim to sinlessness (see below, pp. 58–9). In part this is because while 1 John does hold firmly on to God's loving and life-giving action on 'our behalf (4:9,14), it is less

---

[54] Houlden, *Ethics*, 8–9.
[55] E. Stegemann, 'Kindlein, hütet euch vor den Götterbildern', *TZ* 41 (1985), 284–94, sees a reference to the temptation to participate in idol worship in the face of persecution and uses this to interpret the letter as a whole. Schunack, *Briefe des Johannes*, 106 also accepts a literal interpretation, but sees it as part of a later addition to the letter (vv. 14–21), reapplying it in a new setting.
[56] See Houlden, *Ethics*, 15–17 on justification by faith.

interested in the mechanics of that action. Equally there is no sense that moral behaviour might even appear to be directed towards the same goal. Behaviour can in no way, even misconceived, be seen as creating or maintaining a relationship with God; it is rather the fruit and the test of such a relationship and therefore an aspect of it. As we have seen (above, pp. 49–50), the invisible reality of relationship with God and the visible realities of behaviour are interdependent.

One consequence of this potentially fruitful perception is that there is little room for striving. This does not mean that the author has no need to urge his readers on – he does, repeatedly: 'Abide in him'; 'Let us love one another.' Even statements of 'fact' – 'Everyone who loves the begetter also loves the one begotten from him' (5:1) – only need stating because they are not fully realised. That someone might sin and might see a brother sinning (2:1; 5:16) is clearly the fact. Yet theologically there is little room for all this; hence the assurance 'Everyone who has been born of God does not do sin.'

Sinlessness

Whereas other claims to religious experience are assumed valid if authenticated by the life of the believer, there is one claim which is categorically rejected. The claim not to possess sin[57] or not to have sinned (with the emphasis on the subsequent state of being) is not only self-deception, it is a mockery of God (1:8–10). Already this stands in tension with the assertion that equal falsity lies in failing to walk in the light while claiming fellowship with God (1:6), for could not one who did walk in the light claim to be free from sin?

That initial paradox, not unique in the New Testament, is sharpened by the conjunction of 5:16–17 (if anyone sees a brother sinning) with 5:18 (we know that anyone born of God does not sin). The second element of the paradox is filled out in chapter 3 by a number of affirmations – everyone who abides in

---

[57] The Greek 'to have (*echein*) sin' could be understood as 'bearing the guilt of sin' (so Brown, *Epistles*, 205–6).

him or who has been born of God does not do sin, and indeed cannot sin, while the one who does do sin is of the devil (3:6,8,9).[58]

A history of such an affirmation of sinlessness is easy to trace. From an eschatological perspective within Judaism the freedom from sin belongs to the final age (*T. Levi* 19:9; 1QS 4:21f.); such a perspective reflects an opposition between God and the devil or evil one allowing of no middle ground. In the final conflict the two sides are ranged against each other with members of their forces committed to one side or the other. Inevitably, where the sense of the imminence of that conflict is strong, there is no room for the wavering or uncommitted, even less for the renegade; no forgiveness for anyone who 'goes over' to the other side. Such a mood is reflected elsewhere in the early Christian tradition and leads to difficulties in coping with the fact of sin (see p. 108).

Where there is a strongly realised eschatology, with the sense that the blessings of the age to come are already experienced in the present, freedom from sin as one of those blessings can be claimed for the present. Inasmuch as that eschatology is not totally realised but some hope is reserved for the future, freedom from sin may be modified by a 'not yet' which allows for the reality of actual sin. While the 'not yet' is to be found in 1 John (3:2), there is a strongly 'realised' understanding of religious experience with, as we have seen, a tendency towards the irreversibility of images such as being born from God. Of course no New Testament, or Christian, writing can avoid wrestling with the meaning of an assertion that in Jesus Christ sin and the powers of evil have in some way been defeated or negated, while those who make that victory their own continue to live 'normal' lives in this world.

Before we see how 1 John fits into this framework we need to ask again what the letter means by 'sin' and by the plural 'sins' (see above, p. 52). The plural is used of sins forgiven (1:9; 2:12; 3:5) or propitiated (2:2; 4:10; at 1:7 'every sin' has a plural sense), but also to be confessed (1:9), which implies their

---

[58] On this and what follows see J. L. Bogart, *Orthodox and Heretical Perfectionism in the Johannine Community as Evident in the First Epistle of John*, SBLDS 33 (Missoula, 1977).

present reality. The singular 'sin' could be interpreted as a power, as encompassing but greater than individual acts of wrongdoing. Even if this were the case, it is not clear that 1 John is saying that Christians may, indeed do, commit and must confess their sin*s* but cannot belong totally to the sphere of sin. In 1:8 the claim not to have *sin* (singular) is rejected while the verb 'to sin' is used in both contexts, of what is the case and of what cannot be the case for Christians.[59] Moreover, to do *sin* is equated with doing righteousness and virtually identified with loving a brother (3:7–10) and so must refer to individual acts, as must the sin which a brother may be caught committing (5:16). Thus while it is true that sin does belong to the sphere which opposes God, the dilemma cannot be solved by a contrast between the singular 'sin' and the plural 'sin*s*'.

Neither can we explain the tension simply as a polemic against the supposed claims of the opponents, as if the author were countering a perfectionism that led to moral indifference – first denying their assertion that because sin had been defeated for us such 'sins' as we might commit are of no significance and need no confession, but secondly also asserting against their practice that when such moral indifference results in unconcerned 'sinful' behaviour (including hatred of the brethren), all claims to religious experience are proved null and void.[60] If there is polemic behind the argument (as may be suggested by 'deceive' in 3:7), it is unlikely to have created an apparently important element in the author's theology.

Some have argued that 'sin' means 'unbelief', as is the case in the Fourth Gospel;[61] the argument would then be that we cannot deny that we have belonged to the sphere of sin, that is of unbelief, for to deny that would be to deny the transformation God's sending of his Son has made possible. Equally the sin believers cannot by definition commit while rightly

---

[59] The Greek style of 1 John does not support seeing a distinction between the use of the perfect tense at 1:10 (the claim not 'to have sinned' which is excluded) and the present at 5:16 (the brother who 'sins').

[60] For the problem in recreating the opponents' views from the letter and then using them to interpret the letter see above, pp. 15–16; on such a view of the opponents see n. 43 above.

[61] So Heise, *BLEIBEN*, 149f.

claiming to be born of God is that of unbelief. The sin unto death of 5:17 is that which a brother cannot commit, lack of belief and a refusal to believe in Jesus.[62] However, this solution does not take sufficiently seriously the appeals to Jesus as righteous and as the one who came to take away sins and to destroy the deeds of the devil, or the repeated concern with sin characteristic of the letter which suggests that something else is in mind than the question of unbelief, which is dealt with elsewhere.

The tension can be explained within a theological framework: the believer is 'simul justus et peccator', at once justified and a sinner; in Christ freed from sin, yet before God a sinner in need of justification. The believer's whole existence must be a unity of walking in the light *and* living on the basis of forgiveness, so that it is God's free act and the gift of forgiveness which are the object of trust, and not oneself or one's own achievements.[63] Alternatively, the sinlessness which is God's offer is imperfectly realised in the believer here and now: 'the fact that he has been begotten of God excludes the possibility of his committing sin as an expression of his true character, though actual sins may, and do, occur, in so far as he fails from weakness to realize his true character'.[64]

Valuable as these insights are, it is clear that the 'perfectionist' assertions of chapter 3 must be set within the dualistic scheme which opposes 'the Son of God' or 'God' with 'the devil', doing righteousness with doing sin, the children of God with the children of the devil. The eschatological note sounded in the identification of sin with lawlessness is a realised eschatology. We have already noted the potential determinism in such a scheme, which surfaces in the claim that 'because his seed remains in him, [and] he cannot sin because he has been born of God' (3:9b) (see above, pp. 34–5). It is a dualism

---

[62] So D. M. Scholer, 'Sins Within and Sins Without. An Interpretation of 1 John 5:16–17', in *Current Issues in Biblical and Patristic Interpretation*, ed. G. Hawthorne (Michigan, 1975), 230–46.

[63] So H. Braun, 'Literar-Analyse und theologische Schichtung im ersten Johannesbrief', *ZTK* 48 (1951), 262–92, 277.

[64] A. E. Brooke, *A Critical and Exegetical Commentary on the Johannine Epistles*, ICC (Edinburgh, 1912), 89.

which could appear timeless and static, with two groups within humankind 'from the beginning' (3:8), those born of God who do not and cannot sin, and those born of the devil. It is highly possible that here 1 John is reworking a source or tradition exhibiting such a fixed dualism, for the passage yields a series of couplets which betray a remarkable parallelism of structure and thought ('Everyone who does righteousness is born of him; everyone who does sin also does lawlessness', 2:29b and 3:4a; continued in 3:6; 3:7a and 8a; 3:9a and 10b).[65] In his use of it, however, the sense of timelessness is broken by the insertion of 3:8b, 'the Son of God was manifest for this purpose, in order to destroy the deeds of the devil'. This implies that a new situation has been introduced, whether this new situation breaks the deadlock between the two powers or in fact creates the dualism because prior to that time the devil held sway. The problems posed by the scheme and by his adoption of it are not answered (see above, pp. 36–7), for he is using it not to develop its consequences but to affirm the assured position of the community and to point to the life-pattern which must ensue. Whatever he means by sin, and whether or not it extends beyond the absence of mutual love, his concern with the inner life of the community and his use of a dualistic scheme possibly not of his own devising are the essential reference points for understanding what is said about sin in chapter 3.

Elsewhere sin fits into a different setting. Forgiveness of sins belongs to the past along with victory over the evil one and knowledge gained of the Father (2:12–14); forgiveness is 'through his name', a possible but far from certain reference to baptism. Yet forgiveness is also a present reality, even for members of the community. The normal pattern is to confess sins, perhaps in a public, community setting, and to seek to live in the light, and so to receive cleansing from sin (1:7,9). Such forgiveness is variously expressed as coming from God (who is the one described as faithful and just in 1:9) or from the blood

---

[65] This original insight goes back to E. v. Dobschütz, 'Johanneische Studien I', *ZNW* 8 (1907), 1–8, and has been widely followed.

of Jesus (1:7), probably a general reference to the continual efficacy of the death of Jesus rather than a specific reference to eucharist or baptism.[66] Thus cleansing is a present activity just as we have seen that Jesus is significant for what he *is* in the present (above, p. 56). This is why true Christian life in forgiveness demands the confession of Jesus as 'coming by' the blood (5:6). Other images are also used, suggesting the author has no fixed idea of the significance of Jesus for forgiveness. Thus Jesus is also an 'intercessor' (a paraclete) before the Father on behalf of believers who sin (2:1); the image is not developed further in the Epistle, but the term seems to imply a courtroom setting either with an advocate for the defence or with an intercessor making an appeal for mercy. The idea is one that has Jewish roots; both Abraham and Moses intercede before God in the Old Testament, while in later Jewish literature the angel Michael often has this role. Probably we should not try to tie down 1 John too precisely, and although the letter shares the word with the Fourth Gospel, there is no explicit link with the latter's presentation of the spirit as 'another Paraclete' (John 14:16). Another image comes in 2:2, 'he is a *hilasmos* for our sins' (so also 4:10): the word has been variously translated as 'propitiation', 'expiation', 'atonement' or, more generally, a means of dealing with sin. It is a term which in the Greek translation of the Old Testament has both a technical cultic or sacrificial meaning, as in relation to the Day of Atonement (Lev. 25:9), and a general reference to God's forgiveness (Ps. 130:4). Although it is not a term used directly in the New Testament, related ones are: in Heb. 9:5 and 2:17 the setting is explicitly the Jewish Day of Atonement, while in Rom. 3:25 the following 'by his blood' points to a sacrificial but more generalised understanding. In Judaism at this time the death of the Maccabean martyrs was coming to be understood as a means of reconciliation or 'expiation' (using related vocabulary) for the nation, perhaps offering a model for

---

[66] A reference to the eucharist is found by J. T. Forestell, *The Word of the Cross*, AnBib 57 (Rome, 1974), 189, and one to a baptismal setting by Nauck, *Tradition und Charakter*, 50–4.

Christian understanding of Jesus' death.[67] In 1 John, however, there is nothing to demand a sacrificial understanding (other than the independent reference to the blood of Jesus in 1:7), particularly as not only did God *send* (aorist) Jesus as a *hilasmos* (4:10), but he *is* (present) one (2:2) – past act and present reality. In all the emphasis is probably on the reconciliation thus made possible and not on any precise model of its method.[68]

Denial of guilt or of sinfulness, or the refusal to acknowledge misbehaviour as 'sin', may indeed have been a temptation for the community – hence the antithetical style of 1:8–10, 'If we say ... '; this would be hardly surprising in view of the tendencies to assurance and to realised eschatology which we have emphasised. The author's concern, however, is not simply the recognition of the presence of sin, but the necessity of confession and of seeking forgiveness (1:9), which are essential parts of the acknowledgement of what God has done and of his demands.[69] Such seeking, even on behalf of a fellow believer, carries the assurance of forgiveness (5:16: it is not clear whether in 'he will give him life' the subject is the one praying or God, although ultimately it must be God).

Certainly there remains a tension if not contradiction in what 1 John says about sin; this is obvious in the last part of chapter 5, where the passage first distinguishes between sin which is or is not 'unto death' (16–17), but then asserts that the one born from God does not sin (without modification) (18). Here it does seem most probable that the sin unto death is the denial of belief or schism from the community, for parallel ideas are found elsewhere in the New Testament (Heb. 6:4f.); however, the unequivocal assertion of the inability of the one

---

[67] 4 Macc. 17:22; see M. de Jonge, 'Jesus' Death for Others and the Death of the Maccabean Martyrs', in *Text and Testimony*, ed. T. Baarda et al. (Kampen, 1988), 142–51.

[68] However, the New English Bible translation 'remedy for defilement' brings in ideas that are not necessarily present. On the link with intercession see Forestell, *Word of the Cross*, 18, and on the use of the theme in contemporary Christian thought the study of Hebrews by B. Lindars in this series. For a full and clear discussion of the term in the context of 1 John see S. Lyonnet and L. Sabourin, *Sin, Redemption and Sacrifice. A Biblical and Patristic Study* (Rome, 1970), 148–55.

[69] So Braun, 'Literar-Analyse', 265–6.

born from God to sin does not simply refer to this sin but returns to the dualist scheme of chapter 3, as is shown in the ensuing contrast with the evil one in whose power lies the world (18–19). Thus the tension lies in 1 John's use, particularly in the second part of the letter, of a strongly dualist scheme which is not fully integrated with other aspects of his thought; it may be theologically provocative along lines suggested above (p. 61), but these lines are not 1 John's.

Love of God and love in the community

The 'visible realities' of the 'tests of life' are the criteria for testing an 'invisible reality', the relationship with God;[70] at the same time the external pattern of life is the fruit of the invisible reality. The argument can move from the test to the certainty of the inner reality (2:3) or from the inner reality to the certainty of the external behaviour (3:9): 'everyone who remains in him [invisible reality] does not sin [visible reality]; everyone who sins [visible reality] has not seen him or known him [invisible reality]' (3:6). We need not suppose from this that the invisible can be reduced in meaning to the visible, that in the last resort being begotten of God has no other content than loving a brother, a moral attitude. Rather the former is the source of the latter;[71] it is because the one who abides in God does not sin that not sinning is an *unavoidable* and not just a *possible* test of abiding in God.

At times the distinction between invisible and visible realities becomes blurred; being or walking in the light or in the darkness belong to both (1:6–7; 2:9–11; see above, p. 53). In 3:3 an apparently parallel formulation, 'he who has this hope in him sanctifies himself', cannot be broken down into internal and external reality (so also 3:4,7).[72] Sinning or not sinning may also belong to both spheres since they can both test an invisible reality (3:6) and constitute a claim that needs testing

---

[70] The terms are those used by Vellanickal, *Divine Sonship*, 242.   [71] *Ibid.*, 231–2.

[72] Vellanickal preserves his scheme by arguing (unconvincingly) that 'has this hope in him', 'is righteous' and 'does iniquity' in these verses are 'interior realities' (*ibid.*, 242).

(1:8). Thus the invisible and visible realities are not just interdependent but in some sense co-extensive.

This interdependence and unity are nowhere clearer than in the theme of love – the theme which has been seen by commentators old and new as the heart of this the 'Epistle of Love'.[73] Certainly statistically the theme is dominant, the noun coming 18 and the verb 28 times and so being the most common 'technical' words of the letter; however, they are not evenly distributed, two-thirds of all occurrences coming in 4:7–5:3, while the uncompromising hostility shown to the schismatics and the probable inward restriction of love for one another have led many to balk at the epithet. Perhaps of chief importance is that through this one theme 1 John can speak of God's relationship with believers, believers' relationship with God and their relationship with one another. It illustrates best the flowing spiral of thought and argument so characteristic of 1 John (see above, p. 22), and on a wider canvass poses more sharply and fruitfully than any other biblical writing the question of the relation between love of God and love of neighbour.[74]

Even on 'love' 1 John's thought is not systematic, but it comes closest to being so in the section 4:7–5:3. In this passage there is little sense of polemic and even the negative statements in vv. 8 (the one who does not love) and 20 (the one who claims to love God while hating a brother) probably serve to sharpen the argument of the section rather than to pillory opponents. Here in all love the priority remains with God and with God's love for 'us' shown specifically (aorist tense) in the sending of his Son (4:10). This is not only the source of Christian love and its obligation (4:11,19) but actually defines love for us. It is only a step further to say 'God is Love' (4:9,16). Although much quoted and hailed as the goal and sum of Johannine

---

[73] So St Augustine in the Prologue to his *Ten Tractates on the Epistle of John* says that the author has much to say and nearly all of it about love; in recent times A. Feuillet, *Le Mystère de l'amour*, exploring the theme of love in the Gospel and Epistle, sees 1 John as having the last and most profound word to say in the declaration 'God is Love' (180).

[74] So J. L. Coppens, 'La Doctrine biblique sur l'amour de Dieu et de prochain', *ETL* 40 (1964), 252–99.

theology,[75] this is no speculative reflection on or definition of
God. It is true that it says more than 'God loves' (alongside
other activities) and something very different from 'Love is
God' (see below, p. 79); yet it is rooted in God as experienced,
and is directed towards the inescapable conditions for those
who claim to continue to experience God. It is surely right to
draw the conclusion, as is often done, that the saying means
not just that God loves but that all God's activity is loving
activity, but 1 John is more concerned with the conclusion that
love must characterise those who claim fellowship with this
God. In v. 8 the affirmation explains the previous such
assertion, while in v. 16 it is followed by one. Grayston usefully
compares the Jewish *Shema* (Deut. 6:4), 'which does not exist to
provide information about the unity of God but sets down the
conditions on which God will benefit his people' (p. 124).

The love which God's nature calls for in response can be
simply to love (without an object: 4:8,19; see 16, 'to abide in
love'), but this is more usually defined as love for a brother
(one another) or as love for God. In contrast to the Fourth
Gospel, where the disciples are said or called only to love Jesus,
believers do (or should) love God (4:20–1). At times 1 John
speaks of 'the love of God', and it is ambiguous as to whether
this is love for God (as in 5:3) or the love which comes from
God (as in 4:9).[76] While such ambiguity is too characteristic of
this author to be read as theological subtlety, the letter does
affirm both that loving behaviour is the visible reality which
establishes the invisible reality of divine indwelling, and
equally that it is in love that God is present in and among
believers (invisible reality).

Love is by definition, especially against an OT background,
dynamic rather than static. While God's act of love is complete, this love which flows from God and finds expression in
believers' love for God as well as for one another also invites
further completion. The language of perfection or completion,

---

[75] Feuillet, *Le Mystère de l'amour*, 180–2.

[76] 2:5; 3:17 and 4:12. See J. L. Coppens, 'Agape et Agapan dans les lettres johanniques', *ETL* 45 (1969), 125–7, who prefers 'love for God' here in disagreement with
M. de Jonge.

a common NT theme (Matt. 5:48; 1 Cor. 2:6; 13:10; Phil. 3:12), is used only of love in 1 John (2:5; 4:12,17,18). Yet such perfection can be realised here and now, in obedience to God and in mutual love, and in anticipation of full confidence before God. Again it is ambiguous whether the love that is thus completed is God's love for us or our love for God (see above), and the ambiguity is perhaps best left unresolved.

New elements are added when we look further beyond this key passage. God's love for us (probably so, but literally the more ambiguous 'love the Father has given us') is also expressed in our (believers') right to be called children of God (3:1). At 3:16 Jesus' offering of himself is appealed to as declaring the meaning of love: in contrast to the Fourth Gospel, Jesus' love is spoken of in this verse only, and perhaps here too the focus is more on that as an expression of God's love (see the following 'love of God' in v. 17). The theme of commandment (not dominant in 4:7–5:3 except at the very end, 4:21 and 5:2) is joined with that of love. Mutual love is to be exercised because it is the command given by God and part of the founding proclamation of the community (3:11,28) (see above, p. 52 on the commandment (s)).

Two formulae are used for mutual love: loving 'one another' is used with the first person plural ('we', 'let us') or with reference to the command (3:11,23; 4:7,11,12); loving 'the brother' (sing.) is used almost exclusively in the formula 'he who ... ' or 'everyone who ... ' (2:10; 3:10; 4:20,21).[77] The two different forms may reflect two different traditions, particularly since the Gospel knows only the 'love one another' formula (John 13:34; 15:12,17), but the primary meaning is probably the same. It is true that in 4:21, 'the one who loves God should also love his brother', we hear an echo of Jesus' 'Great Commandment' (love of God and love of 'neighbour': Mark 12:28–34), and this might suggest that it is as a fellow human being that a brother (or neighbour) is to be loved.[78] Yet

[77] The exception is 3:14, where the context demands the form 'we love the brethren' (pl.); the following verse returns to the 'everyone who (hates) a brother' form.

[78] So J. A. T. Robinson, *The Priority of John* (London, 1985), 329–39, esp. 332–3. The word translated 'neighbour' in the command of Lev. 19:18, which lies behind the NT formulations, is also represented elsewhere in the Greek OT by 'brother', and

within 1 John's whole message it is the love experienced within the community, love for the one who is also born of God (5:2), which is at stake. This appears to make the primary concern the cohesion of the community; only in the single demand that such love be manifested in sharing one's physical goods with a brother in need (3:17–18) is such love saved from being nothing more than the continuing membership of the community. This does appear to make love an agent of exclusivism, of separation from those outside. Inevitably the circumstances of the early church meant that for all NT writers, and not just the Johannine authors, loving relations within the community would have priority over and be more realistic than with those outside (for instance Rom. 13:8; 1 Pet. 1:22); yet the Johannine preoccupation with mutual love has rightly been seen as reflecting a particularly strong sense of internal cohesion and external disregard.[79] Clearly a number of factors have contributed to this emphasis, including perhaps the experience of hostility from outsiders and, for 1 John especially, the shock of the schism which split the community and set a question mark against their previous apparent unity. There may be too, although this is far from obvious, a reaction against alternative ('gnostic') claims to 'love' which had little concrete expression – hence the affirmation that full (loving) participation in the life of the community is the ultimate test of all claims to religious experience. If such claims lead to isolationism or schism, they are proved false.[80]

In locating a theological source for this view of love we must look to the dualism of the letter and its attitude to the world. The world, which stands over against the community, both is the source of hatred (3:13) and cannot be the object of love (2:15); the community is the sphere of love (4:20), while love is that which takes place in, and only in, the community (4:16).

the two, 'neighbour' and 'brother', can be used in parallel as at *T. Reub.* 6:9, 'that each do truth towards his neighbour and has love for his brother'.
[79] The bibliography for this is large; see, for example, H. Montefiore, 'Thou shalt Love thy Neighbour as Thyself', *NovT* 5 (1962), 157–70; C. R. Bowen, 'Love in the Fourth Gospel', *JR* 13 (1933), 39–49; M. Rese, 'Das Gebot der Bruderliebe in den Johannesbriefen', *TZ* 41 (1985), 44–58.
[80] See Schnackenburg, *Johannesbriefe*, 250 on 1 John 4:20.

There is no middle ground – not to love is to hate, and to hate is
to put oneself outside the community and outside the sphere of
life (3:14–15). To hate, i.e. not to love, is to be a murderer, and
it is hatred only of a brother which is in view. This dualism
finds its clearest expression in chapter 3, which develops the
story of the murderous hatred of one brother for another, Cain
for Abel, in the setting of the opposition between God and the
devil, life and death. It is in this context that the author warns
them of the hatred of the world (3:13); if we start from the
theme of the hatred of brothers we might decide that those who
hated their brothers were the schismatics who left the community and who are now labelled as 'the world'. Yet there is no
reason to limit the 'world' to them, for it is part of a more
comprehensive dualist pattern. So too hatred belongs to the
sphere of darkness (2:9–11), which does itself have a near to
demonic force (see p. 81). Yet for all this believers are urged
only 'not to love' the world, and not explicitly 'to hate' it.
Although parallels are often drawn between the Johannine
theme of love and the Qumran restriction of 'love of fellow' to
fellow member of the community, 1 John does not parallel the
Qumran injunction to 'love all the sons of light – and hate all
the sons of darkness' (1QS 1:9–11).

Thus love brings together the 'objective' experience of God
and the visible life of those who believe. It emphasises too that
the sphere of religious life for 1 John is not individual but
communal; this is true despite the individualistic nature of the
dominant images of 1 John such as birth from God and the
absence of familiar corporate images like 'the body (of Christ)',
the church, Israel (see above, pp. 43, 47). Yet while this means
love is as much a bond of unity as an ethical attitude, it is not
rooted in the divine unity of love. Here there is a significant
difference from the Gospel, where love first of all characterises
the relationship between Father and Son, and then Son and
disciples (John 15:9; 17:23–6), a difference which is only
overcome when the thought of the Gospel is seen as presupposed by the Epistle.[81] Rather 1 John's insight must be seen on

---

[81] As it is by Feuillet, *Le Mystère de l'amour*, 108, 194 (rooting love in the Trinity and
seeing this as necessitating treating Gospel and Epistle as complementary), and
also by Vellanickal, *Divine Sonship*, 308, 315.

its own terms – love is the decisive commandment and necessary sign of belonging to the community, because love is how
this community have experienced God-towards-them.

JESUS IN TRADITION AND FAITH

At the heart of the letter and of its concern with eternal life
stands the affirmation, 'Who is the liar except the one who
denies that Jesus is the Christ; this is the antichrist, the one
who denies the Father and the Son' (2:22). Two key themes
emerge from this verse: first, the importance of confession or
'faith that' – Jesus is not only the direct object of faith (5:10)
but may also be misinterpreted or wrongly believed.
Secondly, right faith in and about Jesus is inseparable from
experience of and relationship with God as 'Father'. Dispute
about the 'that' of faith is not, as it can never be, an abstract
or self-enclosed debate about detail.

In 2:22 the emphasis is that Jesus is 'the Christ' (*ho christos*,
so also 5:1). This could be seen as an affirmation of Jesus as
the Messiah (=Greek *christos*) of Jewish expectation, as at
John 7:41 (see also Acts 2:36); the Jesus whose human life-
story can be told is acclaimed as the promised one or the
eschatological king. If the right confession of Jesus as the
Christ belongs to 'that which you have heard from the beginning' (2:24), we might think of the fundamental confession
made at baptism and elsewhere.[82] However, for 1 John Jesus
as the Christ means more than that he is the promised
Messiah. 'Christ' is no longer just an epithet or title but is
part of the 'name' of Jesus and has generated related terms
into 1 John's vocabulary, *antichristos* and *chrisma*. Also, of
greater importance than the confession of Jesus as the Christ
is that of Jesus as the Son of God (4:15; 5:5,10; see also 3:8).
Indeed, the two titles are used in apposition to each other and
as virtually interchangeable, so 5:1 is balanced by 5:5 and

---

[82] See Brown, *Epistles*, 352; however, H. F. v. Campenhausen, 'Das Bekenntnis im
Urchristentum', *ZNW* 63 (1972), 210–53, argues that there was no particular
context for confession and it could be used in preaching, exhortation, prayer, debate
and ordinary conversation.

2:22 by 2:23.[83] Although this does not exclude a messianic interpretation – whatever the Jewish background, early Christian sources count 'Son of God' as a messianic title (Acts 8:37) – 1 John uses 'Son' in a more developed sense. When Jesus is referred to as 'the Son' or 'his Son', it is in close conjunction with 'the Father'. 'Everyone who denies the Son, does not have the Father; the one who confesses the Son also has the Father' (2:23; see also 1:3; 4:14). Jesus can be called 'his Son' where a reference to God is only implicit: 1:7; 3:23. The closeness between Jesus as Son and God as Father is such that for the believer experience of one carries with it experience of the other (2:24).

This would seem to point to what might be termed a 'high' christology where Jesus is being brought ever closer to God. Similarly in 5:20, '*This* is the true God and eternal life', '*this*' may refer back to 'Jesus Christ', the immediately preceding words.[84] However, here and elsewhere it seems better to describe 1 John's christology as ambiguous rather than high. Thus 'the one from the beginning' in 2:13–14 may either be Jesus, who is thus declared pre-existent, or be God. Despite the echoes of John 1:1f., it is unlikely that 1 John 1:1f. refers to Jesus as the pre-existent word or *logos* of God (see above, p. 23). While language of the Son as sent by God (4:9,14) or as being manifested (3:8) may imply pre-existence, it may equally only stress the authority of the one 'sent'.[85] The frequent use of 'him' or 'his' (*auton, autou*), where the reference may be to either God or Jesus, reflects a lack of precision in the author's style rather than the assimilation of the identity or role of one to the other. For example in 2:3–6 it is simply unclear whether someone might claim to have known God or Jesus, and whose commandments are being kept.

83 See M. de Jonge, 'Variety and Development in Johannine Christology', in *Jesus: Stranger from Heaven and Son of God* (Missoula, 1977), 193–222.

84 Brown, *Epistles*, 625–6 favours a reference to Jesus and notes that the surprising close association or even identification with eternal life recalls the prologue (1:2) – although I have hesitated to see an explicit reference to Jesus there.

85 Whether 'Son' and 'sending' language implies pre-existence in the Fourth Gospel is much debated; see A. E. Harvey, *Jesus and the Constraints of History* (London, 1982), 154–73 and especially 161–8, who stresses the themes of obedience, reliability,

Particularly obscure is the passage 2:28–3:2. Our knowledge of New Testament teaching might lead us to take 2:28, 'Now, children, abide in *him*, so that if [*he*] is manifested we may have boldness and not be ashamed from *him* at *his* coming [*parousia*]', as a reference to Jesus; he is the one whose coming or parousia is anticipated. Yet in the following verse, 'if you know that [*he*] is righteous, you know that everyone who does righteousness if born of *him*', the final 'him' must be God, of whom believers are always born in 1 John. Does v. 28 then refer to *God's* coming, or has 'he/him' shifted in its reference at some point in the two verses? Chapter 3 starts with an explicit reference to God (the Father), but by the end of the verse ambiguity returns, 'therefore the world does not know us, because it did not know *him*', where we might expect this to be the failure of the world to recognise *Jesus*. V. 2 continues, 'we are now children of *God*, and it is not yet manifested what we shall be. We know that if "it" (or "*he*") is manifested we shall be like *him*, because we shall see *him* as (he) is.' We are left wondering whether 1 John envisages the manifestation of God and believers' conformity to him as a stage further than being his children, or the manifestation of and conformity of believers to Jesus. This is not a high christology, or even an expression of the inseparability of Son and Father in the work of salvation,[86] but a lack of precision in the author's thought; and so we cannot speak with any confidence of Jesus' eschatological role in 1 John.

More certainly 1 John is concerned with what Jesus has done and does do, although again there is a variety of imagery to express this. In laying down his life for *us* he made known love and gave an example to be followed (3:16). The 'mythological' world view implied by 3:8, that the Son of God was manifested to annul or destroy the deeds of the devil, is not developed elsewhere (but see above, pp. 61–2 on this section). In 3:5 he was manifested to 'take away' sins, either a general reference to forgiveness or a more specific one to the

---

authority and unity of purpose. In 1 John the language cannot be pushed for a specific answer to this problem.
[86] As is argued by Vellanickal, *Divine Sonship*, 246f.

removal of the power of sin by the gift of sinlessness.[87] Jesus'
dealing with sin as a *hilasmos* (2:2; 4:10) is only marginally
more precise; as we have seen, sacrificial overtones may be
present but cannot be over-pressed, and Jesus continues to be
(2:2, 'is'), and not just was in his death, such a means of
dealing with sin (see above, pp. 63–4). More generally 2:14
speaks of sins as forgiven 'through his name', while in 1:9, only
two verses after Jesus' blood is described as a source of
cleansing, it is probably God who is 'faithful and just' so as to
forgive and to cleanse (a reference which has links with Exod.
34:6). Despite this last reference, Jesus' significance in relation
to the overcoming of sin is certain, but not integrated into a
single understanding of his person.

As 'paraclete' Jesus continues to act for believers before 'the
Father' when they sin (2:1; see above, p. 63); yet this image too
is not sustained. Believers may also have boldness before God
in the confidence given by their own obedience to his commands (3:21–2), and perhaps, when confidence is lacking, in
the awareness of God's greater knowledge (3:19–20). On the
day of judgement such boldness rests not on their having a
heavenly advocate to speak on behalf of their weakness, but
'because as that one is, so are we in the world' (4:17). The
context here seems to indicate that it is in loving and in
experiencing God's love that believers enter even in this world
into the experience which characterises Jesus.

Jesus' coming and its effects can also be expressed in more
general terms: it was so that 'we might live through him' (4:9;
see also 5:12); he has given the insight that leads to knowledge
of the one who is true (5:20), an affirmation that has a 'gnostic'
ring to it and is only developed elsewhere in the letter in the
debate about claims to know or have known him. Yet, by
contrast, in 4:12 the solution to no one ever having seen God is
not that Jesus has made him known but that 'if we love one
another God abides in us'.

As we have seen, the concern with what Jesus *did* continually
moves towards what he *is* and *does* for us, as believers. Jesus,
'that one' (*ekeinos*), is a model not only in his incarnate life and

87 See Forestell, *The Word of the Cross*, 189.

death in the past (2:6; 3:16), but also in what he *is* now – holy, righteous and without sin (3:3,5,7; 4:17; see above, p. 56).

In all this Jesus, his coming, death and continuing presence are not past events to be looked back to and reflected on; they are important in so far as they become part of contemporary experience. Thus there are no references to his birth, resurrection or exaltation, and even his death is more implied in the concern for what it achieves than proclaimed as a fact to confront, stumble over or struggle to interpret. The same verb, 'to be manifested', can be used of his incarnate life (3:5,8; cf. 1:2; 4:9) as well as of his, presumably very different, future coming (2:28; 3:2. If the subject here is God rather than Jesus, this is all the more surprising). All this is particularly strange in the light of the common interpretation of 1 John as essentially anti-docetic, as affirming the reality of the life and death of Jesus against specific attempts to spiritualise or to evade the offence of that reality. This interpretation rests on a view of the opponents of the letter as advocating such attempts and on the precise meaning of 4:2f. and 5:6f. To these passages we must now turn.[88]

The immediate response to the 'antichrists' is the centrality of the confession of Jesus as the Christ or Son of God (2:18–23; see above). In chapter 4 that affirmation is expanded in an explicitly polemical setting. The only valid confession, here ascribed to the spirit which is of God, is of 'Jesus Christ [as] the one who has come in flesh' (4:2). It is not an affirmation *that* he came in the flesh as against some other form of his coming, for this would require a different grammatical construction in the Greek.[89] It is an acknowledgement of the one who can be so entitled; its reverse (4:3) is simply to fail to confess Jesus. An alternative textual tradition has 'every spirit which "looses" Jesus is not of God'; probably this does not mean to divide him into his divinity versus his humanity but to dissolve Jesus of all

---

88 See above, pp. 14–15 and n. 18. Recent studies tend to be far more cautious than older ones which spoke of 'docetism' or 'gnosticism' and aligned the heresy attacked with those known from the later church. See below.

89 It would require either a 'that' (Greek *hoti*) clause or an accusative and infinitive, a construction which is read by Codex Vaticanus (B) here in an obvious attempt to clarify the issue.

significance just as, rightly believed, he dissolves or destroys the works of the devil (3:8). Although poorly attested, this reading may well be right, for otherwise its origin is difficult to explain.[90]

The point of this more elaborate confession in 4:2 is not clear; presumably the simpler form that Jesus is the Christ or Son of God did not go far enough. Yet the fact that the author is content elsewhere to repeat the simpler formula rather than this expanded one means we should not make the whole of 1 John's christology hang on this single verse. Certainly this verse cannot bear the weight of the argument of older studies that 1 John is concerned to refute the specific belief (a) that in his incarnate life Jesus' humanity was in appearance only and not the common humanity shared by all people; thus he did not truly enter into common human experience, particularly of death; or (b) that the 'incarnation' involved the descent of a divine being (or 'aeon'), the Christ or Son of God, to take human form or to enter into a union with the earthly Jesus which was partial and temporary only, avoiding participation in suffering and death. (See my introduction, p. 14 above.) While both these views were the concern of later doctrinal development, they fit neither the form of the confession in 1 John 4:2 nor what else the letter has to say about Jesus.

The verb in 4:2, 'to come', is used in the letter only of the coming of the antichrists as expected by the community (2:18; 4:3, the present tense used with future force) and of Jesus Christ here and in 5:6. In this verse it is the perfect tense, 'having come in [en] flesh'; in 5:6 Jesus is the one who came (aorist or simple past) 'through water and blood' or, by implication, 'in' (en usually translated 'by') water and blood. This second reference is even more difficult to interpret. Because of the added 'not by (in) the water only but by the water and the blood', it too has been seen as directed against a

---

90 The evidence in its favour is chiefly the Latin versions and church fathers; however, its obscurity would easily lead to its replacement by the straightforward 'does not confess'. If it is not original it may have been added with the heretic Cerinthus in mind, who reputedly made a distinction between the divine Christ and human Jesus: see above, p. 14. For a fuller discussion and list of those scholars who take each side see Brown, *Epistles*, 494–6.

specific heretical view, for example one which denied the genuine experience of death (blood) by the divine element in Jesus Christ while acknowledging his baptism or descent at baptism (water), or which denied that the incarnation was complete and genuine, water *and* blood representing semen *and* seed. Yet here too, as the inability of the interpreters to agree shows, the language of 1 John forbids such precision. It is hard to see how the use of the verb 'came' and the prepositions 'through' or 'in' would be an effective rebuttal of such views, while the author would surely not want to affirm that the divine came upon Jesus at baptism (rather than at birth). The following verses (6b–8) introduce the spirit and speak of spirit, water and blood as three witnesses, and so do little to clarify the situation; a consistent meaning for water and blood is hard to establish and one wonders whether this new theme has been added by word association (see further, pp. 48–9).

Elsewhere flesh appears only in a negative sense (2:16, the desire of the flesh), while water is not used at all; the blood of Jesus, however, is more important, pointing to the (sacrificial?) understanding of Jesus' death as a continuing source of cleansing from sin (1:7). It may be that Jesus' role in relation to sin, which we have already recognised as an important concern for 1 John, is at issue in 4:2f. and 5:6f. Water too is an obvious image of cleansing, whether or not there is a specific reference to baptism either as prescribed by Jesus as a means of forgiveness or as undergone by him in self-identification with humankind, both of which are possible interpretations but hardly required by the text. Both passages would then declare that to confess Jesus as the Christ or Son of God is to confess that as the one sent by God he is the source of forgiveness, particularly in virtue of his death. Beyond this we may hesitate to go – and this includes speculating about the beliefs of his opponents. Since the author does not describe them for us, and is more concerned to detail right confession (4:2) than wrong (4:3), we are ill equipped to reconstruct; the 'not only … but also' of 5:6 is probably his emphasis (as it is at 2:2) and not a reference to the 'only' of the opponents' beliefs. The advantage of this interpretation of the texts is that it does provide a bridge between the confessional affirmations and the statements about what 1 John does; it also confirms our impression that 1 John is little concerned with the 'thatness' of Jesus' life.

Another aspect of this tension between the expressed concern for right belief in Jesus and the lack of clear reflection about that belief is the oft-noted theocentricity of 1 John. Admittedly this is particularly marked when seen in comparison with the Gospel, and it may be that it is the christocentricity of the Gospel which is more worthy of note. Thus God is light in 1 John (1:5), while this is said of Jesus in John (1:5ff.; 3:19; 8:12); abiding is exclusively christocentric in the Gospel (John 6:56; 15:4–7) but not in 1 John (4:12,15–16; see above, p. 41); knowledge of God is dependent on knowledge of Jesus in John (14:7; 17:3), while the Epistle speaks of it as a direct relationship or experience (4:6–8). Imagery of the believer as possessing fellowship with God, being born and thus a child of God or simply 'of God' is fundamental to the thought of the Epistle but of far less significance in the Gospel (see above, pp. 37, 40–1). The reverse of this is that over half of the references to 'Jesus' or 'Christ' come following the verbs 'to believe' or 'to confess', and only 'Son (of God)' is used more regularly outside this context.[91] Thus Jesus' present meaning for believers is important and so is his place within the tradition of the community, but it is the relationship with God which really defines the continuing existence of the community and its members.

What insights, then, does 1 John offer into the nature of God and God's dealings with humankind? Here we need only bring together themes which have been explored more fully elsewhere. God is the focus of believers' experience, and much that is said about God is within the framework of the believer–God relationship. The discussion above about the various expressions of that relationship has therefore already included its 'God' side. God is not only a partner in that relationship, but is its initiator. That believers are called 'children of God' is

---

[91] Seven (8 including 5:6, which implies a confessional context) out of the 12 uses of 'Jesus' come after the verb 'to believe' or 'to confess', as do 4 (5) out of 8 occurrences of 'Christ', and 8 out of 22 of 'Son'.

evidence of God's love given to them (3:1); God is the begetter
of those born from him (5:1); God is the giver of the spirit (3:24;
4:13) as also the sender of the Son. That confession of sins is
met by forgiveness is due to God's character as faithful and just
(1:9). Although no one has even seen God, more can be said:
God is love (4:8,16) and God is light (1:5). As we have already
noted with regard to the former, the author does not say
'Love/light is God' or (although this is true) 'God loves/gives
light'; his concern is not so much to speak of the nature and
being of God, as of God as known and experienced. The two
clearly belong together, but the author's main focus is the
latter: those who claim fellowship with God must judge their
lives by the self-revelation of and the proclamation about God;
love is not an optional extra for those who claim to know God
but is intrinsic to all experience of God; light has a moral force
and the one who claims fellowship with God cannot remain
marked by darkness. The parallel drawn earlier with the *Shema*
(p. 67 above) together with the contexts of the sayings in 1
John also points to the corporate setting of these affirmations
(fellowship with one another in 1:6, love for one another in
4:7); that God is light or love does not mean that fellowship
with God is achieved by the solitary search for enlightenment
or mystical adoration, nor does it distance God into the
absolute or into philosophical speculation. The assertion that
there is no darkness in God who is the light does, but perhaps
not deliberately, exclude the possibility that in the divine there
is a mixture of light and darkness or that God is the source of
darkness. This will lead us to the dualism of the letter (below,
pp. 80–3).

God is also the Father, usually named as such alongside the
Son; '*our (your)* Father' is never used, although in 3:1 it is a
consequence of the Father's love that 'we should be called
children of God'. Yet if we were to ask of 1 John 'Who is this
God?', 'What has been the past activity of this God among
humankind?', we would receive little information beyond 'the
one who sent his Son among us'.

GOD AND THE WORLD: ELECTION AND DUALISM

As has become repeatedly clear, 1 John works with a dualist pattern which marks both its thought to differing degrees and also its structure. The antithetical statements which form the backbone of the letter allow of two contrasting possibilities with no middle term: either one loves or one hates, one is born of God or is not of God. How thorough-going is this dualism, and what are its roots? Distinctions are often made between ethical dualism (where two contrasting patterns of behaviour divide humankind), cosmic dualism (where there are two opposing camps of supernatural powers), metaphysical dualism (two absolutely opposed divine principles) and eschatological dualism (a contrast between the present age and the age to come).[92] Clearly these are not mutually exclusive and cannot always be neatly distinguished: for example one, a cosmic dualism, may be a mythicised form of another, an ethical dualism.

An absolute dualism is foreign to the monotheism of the Jewish and Christian traditions. However, the intertestamental period saw the development of dualist patterns in Jewish thought with varying attempts to reconcile this dualism with the absolute sovereignty of God. Indeed it is this inherent tension which leads many to argue that such dualism could not develop purely from the Old Testament traditions but owes something to foreign, perhaps to Zoroastrian, thought.[93] Moreover, dualism was not only to be found in Jewish thought at this period. Greek ideas which could denigrate the material in contrast to the spiritual or non-physical have often been seen as an influence behind the developed dualism of gnostic systems and even of the Fourth Gospel.

The dualism of 1 John is easily sketched. The proclamation heard and made is that 'God is light and in him there is no darkness' (1:5). This is no abstract or metaphysical definition

---

[92] A dualism between soul or spirit and body is clearly not in view for 1 John.
[93] See H. Ringgren, 'Qumran and Gnosticism', and M. Mansoor, 'The Nature of Gnosticism in Qumran', in *The Origins of Gnosticism*, ed. U. Bianci (Leiden, 1967), 379–88, 389–400.

of God: it is God-made-known, God-towards-humankind. Darkness is that which is utterly opposed to God and to light; it has no place in God – there are not two contradictory principles mixed together in the supreme divine being – and we might suppose, although it is not stated, that God is not responsible for darkness so understood. Darkness and light also express two contradictory possibilities of behaviour (1:6f.), but walking in the light is not simply 'in the right' or by illumination, or doing deeds that are not ashamed to be seen. It is living in conformity with the light that is revealed of God. Thus it is more than just an ethical dualism. The ethical is expressed in the contrast between loving and hating (2:9) or between doing righteousness and doing sin (3:4f.), which are mutually exclusive alternatives with no third way, but the ethical points to something more, to the source of such behaviour or being.

Thus, as we have seen, light is identified with God; darkness, although not explicitly identified with an opposing force, does have active power. In 2:11 it is darkness which has blinded the eyes of those who walk in darkness; the allusion there to Isa. 6:10 points to that blinding as a quasi-personal activity – darkness has almost assumed a demonic identity.[94] In chapter 3 the division between people reflects an opposition between God and the devil or evil one – some are born of God and are the children of God, others are of the devil or children of the devil, and there is no median group (see above, pp. 35–6).

Yet this apparently absolute dualism is not maintained; we have seen (pp. 39–40) how the contrast can also be between God and the world (4:5), and that the world, like the darkness, is passing away (2:8,17). Since the world is not thoroughly demonised (see below, pp. 83–4), merely introducing the world as the opposite to God ensures that we are not dealing with an absolute metaphysical dualism. We have also discovered an unresolved tension in 1 John's thought. At times it

---

94 In Isaiah it is implicitly God who is responsible for the blinding of the eyes of those who hear the prophet's message; the verse is quoted in John 12:40, where it is either God or Jesus. In making the subject 'darkness' 1 John adopts a more dualist scheme which does have other NT and Jewish parallels. See J. M. Lieu, 'Blindness in the Johannine Tradition', *NTS* 34 (1988), 83–95.

does seem that humankind consists of two predetermined groups 'from the beginning' (in company with the devil's sinning, 3:8) and that the choices they make – believing and responding (4:6, see p. 39), loving, sinning (see p. 62), leaving the community (2:19, see p. 37) – are but the inevitable expression of this nature. This lack of clarity is a result of 1 John's interest not in the past, pre-Christian experience of believers but in what they now are, and of the letter's consequent failure to explore what is involved in the call to and decision for faith – the dualism of decision often found in the Fourth Gospel has no place in 1 John. This, together with the static imagery used of Christian experience or status, means the present reality can be read as a pre-existing or predetermined reality; it can seem, and 1 John does not guard against this, that what is now true has always been so, even if only in potential. However, there is enough to show that this is not the whole picture for 1 John. The dualism is modified – there is a future dimension, the darkness is passing away, the Son of God appeared to annul the deeds of the devil, the evil one has been conquered. This is not an equal and eternal struggle but one in which the result has already been declared. To this extent there is also a modified, eschatological dualism: that darkness is passing away suggests a sequential order so that darkness (past and present) is contrasted with light (future but already present). The contrast between remaining in death or having passed from death to life (3:14) may be a contrast between two present possibilities of existence or between the present and the future proleptically anticipated.

The two spirits, the spirit of truth and the spirit of error (4:1–6) also hint at a cosmic dualism. Only the former is from God; neither the source nor the nature of the latter is defined except as being 'that of the antichrist'. The spirit of error is not a purely rhetorical, negative example; the author is not saying that what looks like spirit is no spirit if it does not effect right confession. Neither are the spirits here the human spirit or disposition; they are forces from outside which inspire confession and, perhaps, behaviour (3:24). Comparison is often made with the dualism found at Qumran (1QS 3:13–4:26) which has both ethical dimensions and a cosmic setting.[95] There two spirits, the spirit of truth or light and the spirit of perversity, who is associated with darkness, appear at times almost as angelic figures under one or other of whose domain all human-kind is ranged, but at other times as dispositions or influences at war within each individual. They are marked, as are their adherents, by the vices or virtues proper to each; in the same way in 1 John the spirits of truth and of error are characterised by their association with light or with darkness and are recognised by a sign (confession in 1 John, behaviour in the Scrolls). This characterisation and opposition stands in contrast to the use of 'the spirit of truth' in the Fourth Gospel (John 14:17; 15:26; 16:13), where there is no contrast with error (see above, p. 47 and n. 36). Yet 1 John is far from identifying the spirits with angelic or demonic beings, nor is there open conflict between them – although in the identification of the spirit of error as 'that of the antichrist' there is the potential for such thought.

Thus dualism in 1 John is not thoroughly worked through in any one direction. This is because it does not form the starting point for the author, he does not approach reality and experience from a rigid dualist ideology. Rather he uses dualism to express a conviction of the election of the community of believers and to interpret their actual experience. It is unlikely that the experience has created the dualism; a broadly dualist viewpoint, already part of his heritage, has been found to match the experience.

This becomes clear in the attitude to the world (*kosmos*) and its place within the pattern. The world can replace the devil in the opposition to God, most starkly in the contrast between *we* who are of God and *they* who are of the world (4:5). Love for God is incompatible with love for the world, and everything 'in the world' finds its origin not in God but in the world (2:15–16). Taken in isolation this could be read as the total

---

[95] See Charlesworth, 'Critical Comparison' (n. 23 above) and in the same volume, pp. 156–65, M.-E. Boismard, 'The First Epistle of John and the Writings of Qumran', who does see the 'spirit of error' as 'an evil disposition of the human soul' (p. 162).

devaluing of the material world and its separation from God
as the highest good, as in some gnostic thought. Yet this is not 1
John's thought world. Indeed, the world is opposed to God,
recognising neither believers nor him (3:1) and so hating
believers; it is the sphere in which the schismatics (false
prophets) move with some success (4:1,5f.); the world is under
the power of the evil one, who cannot touch *us* (5:18–19). Yet
again it remains unstated whether the world has always been
so, believers having been rescued out of it, or whether the
world has been made into something negative by its rejection
of God and of the community. It is ultimately that which the
community experience as the hostile or indifferent 'world out
there'. Whether we are to think of active hostility or passive
unconcern, of official action or popular reaction, of Jew or of
Greek, or both, for the author it is undifferentiated 'world'.

Because 'the world' is not a theoretical construct but an
experienced reality, there is a very real ambivalence towards it.
The predominant picture is of a negative or opposing power –
victory is not only against the evil one (2:14) but also against
the world (5:4f.). Yet Jesus *is* (present) the means of dealing
with the sins not only of believers but also for the *whole* world
(2:2 – not just an elect part of it). The witness that believers
give is that the Father sent the Son as Saviour of the world
(4:14). Admittedly, this thought is not well integrated into that
of the Epistle as a whole; in 4:9 God sent his Son *into* the world
that *we* might live through him – a related tradition in John
3:16f. makes the world not only the destination of the Son's
sending but also the subject of the salvation thus made
possible. It is possible that these isolated positive references are
relics of a more optimistic evaluation. Yet even if this is so,
their retention betrays the fact that the dominant negative
presentation of the world, like the dualism of the letter, is a
function of the over-riding concern to interpret the community's experience and to affirm their security in faith and in God's
election. We can only guess at the experience which made such
a concern so urgent, but the schism was undoubtedly a key,
though perhaps not the only, factor; in the Fourth Gospel a
similar response has probably been intensified if not provoked

by a sharp break with the Jewish community. A consequence may have been a lack of any real concern for the world; missionary language is used of the appearance of the false prophets who 'have gone out into the world' (4:1) – there is little to suggest that the community would seek to join them.[96]

Certainly the author's opponents have a place within the dualism of the letter. They are the antichrists over against both the Christ and the community who rightly possess a *chrisma*. They are at home in the world and are heard by the world; with them are associated both error and deception (4:6; 2:26). Whatever the actual nature of the conflict, such language declares the impossibility of dialogue, compromise or reconciliation. Within the total dualist pattern of the letter this reads as more than the exaggerated rhetoric of polemic. Aligning opponents, particularly erstwhile partners, with the cosmic forces opposed to God marks a distinctive and perhaps ominous note in the development of attitudes to deviant belief or practice.[97]

If we were to see the opponents as veiled behind the antithetical or debating structure of the letter we could extend this dualist characterisation of the two parties. *They* would be those who walked in darkness, who lied and deceived themselves, in whom neither truth nor his word were to be found, who remained in darkness and were the source of hatred and of death; *we*, the community, would be marked by the opposite characteristics. However, it seems better to see the debate as genuinely directed towards the community; while it may ultimately serve to reinforce the community's characterisation as loving, being in the truth and so on, this does give the dualism a dynamic aspect with an element of what is yet undecided. This is not the dualism of decision for or against faith characteristic of the Fourth Gospel, but a dualism of

---

[96] F. Hahn, *Mission in the New Testament* (London, 1965), 152–63, argues for a far more insular attitude in the Epistles than in the Gospel of John and stresses the use against 'heretics' of missionary expressions; on this see also Lieu, *Second and Third Epistles*, 182–6.

[97] F. Wisse emphasises this in relation to Jude, 'The Epistle of Jude in the History of Heresiology', in *Nag Hammadi Texts in Honour of A. Böhlig*, ed. M. Krause (Leiden, 1972), 133–43.

testing. The community or its members must explore where they stand and discover the full dimensions of the choice they have made. The many-faceted nature of 1 John's dualism creates on the one hand an unmitigated black and white impression of exclusivity, but on the other a division which cuts through the whole of experience, leaving no aspect of life untouched.

The dualism also serves, as we have seen, to highlight the election of the community of believers. This is to return to the theme of assurance that has been a recurring one in our survey of 1 John's thought. Although explicit language of being chosen is not used in 1 John, in contrast to the epithet 'chosen', *eklektos*, in 2 John 1 and 13, the thought continually returns to what *we* are and to God's love for *us* (4:9). The relation between that sense of being chosen and the decision for faith is never expressed, unless we see the whole letter as reflecting or evoking a baptismal setting with a dramatic act of commitment (see above, pp. 7–8). Neither is it related to their past experience: while most commentators assume that the community is predominantly Gentile in origin, or that old divisions have been obliterated,[98] this is an assumption from the total silence of the letter; never are we told from what they have been won, except from death, 3:14. Perhaps more than any other letter in the New Testament, the believers of 1 John are of God, born of God, children of God, and yet totally faceless.

So, too, how they have been chosen is left unclear. Jesus, the Son, must be the key: God's love was manifest in the sending of his Son that we might live through him (4:9); birth from God and victory over the world are both tied to faith in Jesus (5:1,4–5); it is the manifestation of the Son of God which breaks the apparent deadlock between the devil and God (3:8). Yet this linking is left undeveloped and at times is qualified. In 3:14 that 'we love the brethren' may be the grounds for passing from death to life rather than the grounds for knowing that this

---

[98] A thoroughly Jewish audience has also been argued, whether Diaspora (J. A. T. Robinson, 'The Destination and Purpose of the Johannine Epistles', *NTS* 7 (1960–1), 56–65, reprinted in *Twelve New Testament Studies* (London, 1962), 126–38) or Palestinian (O'Neill, *Puzzle of 1 John*).

transition has been made; in 4:4 victory is assured because the one who is in the world (the antichrist) is less than 'the one in you', who may be God rather than Jesus. It is where believers are and not who Jesus is which is the starting point.

PAST AND FUTURE

The response in 1 John to the needs of the present is not to construct a new theology or compelling reinterpretation of the community's faith, but to recall them to their past and to the consequences of what they already hold. This is why for 1 John the past is the past of the community. Its tradition is 'that which you have heard from the beginning', and there is little interest in any other beginning than this (see above, pp. 29–30). Although it was in the sending of the Son that God's love was manifested (4:9), we have found only an ambiguous interest in the past life and death of Jesus with a greater concern for his present significance (see above, pp. 72–5). Jesus too belongs to the past of the community and its tradition; there is no sense of looking back to the foundation of the community and then behind that to what God did in Jesus. Still less do we see God's action in Jesus as part of a prior pattern or preparation. The only explicit appeal to the Old Testament is to the example of Cain and Abel (3:12), precisely as an example and not as a prototype or prophetic model. This does not mean the author has no use for the Old Testament; the Cain narrative may be already in mind in 3:7 and even continue to the end of the chapter; behind 2:11 lies Isa. 6:10; other passages too may go back to OT passages and their exegesis, while, as we have seen, many of the images have Old Testament roots.[99] Yet mostly these belong to the traditions of thought and language the author has inherited and it would matter little if his readers did not recognise them; he does not

---

[99] Thus it is wrong to say, as does D. A. Carson, 'John and the Johannine Epistles', in *It is Written: Scripture Citing Scripture. Essays in Honour of Barnabas Lindars, SSF*, ed. D. A. Carson and H. G. M. Williamson (Cambridge, 1988), 245–64 that 1 John is characterised by 'the absence not only of OT questions but even of many unambiguous allusions to the OT' (p. 256).

argue from the OT or see any need to set God's action with and for this community within any wider canvass.

When we ask what God has yet to do the answer is more ambivalent, but again concentrates on this community of believers. A recurring theme of our exploration has been the realised eschatology of the letter. There is much more awareness of what believers already are than what is yet in store. Some of the images are those which elsewhere in the New Testament belong to the future, such as the victory achieved over the evil one (2:14 and above, p. 28); others are character- istically Johannine – eternal life is a present possession (5:12,13), believers have already passed over from death to life (3:14). Images such as those of abiding or being born of God have a static quality about them which does not look for anything more (see above, pp. 57–8).

Another, and very different, aspect of this is the way the author interprets the present dilemma for the community. The advent (or departure) of the 'schismatics' is given an eschato- logical quality; they are the false prophets or antichrist whose appearance to oppose God and God's faithful people was an expected mark of 'the last hour' (2:18). In this experience the community know that they are living at the crucial moment of testing and decision. At the same time 'the last hour' has no broader significance than for the community of 1 John, and whether that sense extended to the whole of their life is less than certain. It seems most likely that the author has given this interpretation in order to offer an explanation to a perplexed community and to guard against further losses. Thus few further consequences are drawn from the identification, although in principle it opened the way for denial of dialogue with or concern for those deemed heretical.[100]

Alongside all this, however, there are two passages which seem to offer a more traditional future eschatology and have gained for 1 John the assertion that it marks a return to a more

---

[100] As is done in 2 John, although with only implicit eschatological sanction; see also n. 97 above.

primitive eschatology than that of the Gospel.[101] The first of
these is 2:28–3:2, a passage we have already studied in detail
(see above, p. 73). Present abiding in 'him' and the privilege of
being children of God are here seen as preconditions for
something more: boldness and the absence of shame before
'him' 'at his coming' (parousia) and the hope of being like him
when seeing 'him' as 'he' is. The explicit or implicit 'he/him'
throughout this passage means interpretation is far from
certain, but I have argued that the reference is most probably
to *God's* coming and likeness to him. In this case the thought is
not simply that of other Christian writings which look forward
to the return or manifestation of Christ. There are parallels
within the New Testament (Matt. 5:8) and outside, in Jewish
as well as later gnostic sources,[102] both to God's coming and to
the vision of God. The problem here is that it is not easy to see
how the passage fits into the author's thought as a whole; it has
been suggested, but seems unlikely, that the 'if' (*ean*) of 'if he is
manifested' (2:28) may suggest a note of caution, perhaps
about the exact moment but perhaps about the whole idea.[103]
The hope that is offered (3:3) looks not to the future but to the
present, underlining the conformity between God and those
who believe, a conformity to be asserted but also to be
experienced.

The theme of 'boldness' (*parresia*) which this passage introduced is a present experience in prayer in 5:14 and again in
3:21–2. The last comes in a passage which applies to the
present experience and ultimate confidence of believers a
number of other themes that might be associated with future
judgement – before God, condemning, God knows all
(3:19–22). The details of this passage are notoriously difficult
to interpret satisfactorily; the key problem is whether God's
superiority and knowledge of all should be a source of appre-
hension – that God knows more than even we know of our
failings – or of confidence – that God's greater insight offers
more mercy than does all our self-doubt. The tenor of the

---

[101] This is often stated; see, for example, C. H. Dodd, *The Johannine Epistles* (London,
1946), xxxiv–xxxvi; liii–liv.
[102] Brown, *Epistles*, 381, 425.   [103] So Grayston, *Epistles*, 96–7.

passage and of the letter probably favours the latter,[104] for the passage ends on a note of certainty of being heard and of doing right. There is a similar ambivalence about the remaining 'future eschatology' passage, which also introduces the theme of boldness, 4:17–18. Here boldness is the possession of believers on 'the day of judgement', a phrase not otherwise found in the Gospel or letters of John (Matt. 10:15; 11:22,24 etc.). Such boldness is either the full expression or the final goal of love perfected 'among us', yet its basis is that 'as that one is so are we in this world', that is believers' present conformity with Jesus. In fact fear and punishment, which presumably belong to the day of judgement, are excluded by love when fully experienced and realised in the believers' life. Thus the expectation of the future does not qualify the present but establishes its potential richness.

It is wrong to find in 1 John (a return to) a 'primitive' future eschatology, although it may be that the author is picking up the language of this type. Certainly he offers no coherent picture, and it would be equally wrong to try to establish a chronology from 'the last hour' to the day of judgement and to 'his coming'. In different ways these themes are used to say something about the present. While they may be necessary components of our author's thought, and qualify any picture of an unrelieved and static present assurance, they do not change the perspective of the picture.

Faced with schism and perhaps with hostility, 1 John does not take refuge from the present in the hopes of the future. It is easy to see what it does do as a retreat into tradition, a turning in on itself; it can also be recognised as an exploration of a new 'sense of God, and of community'.[105] Weaknesses and strengths are inevitable in any forced response to crisis; both belong to 1 John's contribution to New Testament theology.

---

[104] So Brown, *Epistles*, 459 after a full discussion.

[105] The caution is expressed by E. Schweizer, *Church Order in the New Testament* (London, 1961), 12d–e, pp. 128–30; the quotation comes from the positive evaluation by Perkins, *Epistles*, 101.

THEOLOGY IN 2 AND 3 JOHN?

To draw a theology from one – even two – short and in a sense 'occasional' letter (s) must surely seem a misguided task. The Second and Third Epistles present us with a problem; since the identity of their author with that of the First Epistle remains unproven, we might hesitate to use them to supplement an account of the theology of the latter and equally to use 1 John to give body to their thought. Small wonder that they have often been relegated to footnotes, usually, despite what has just been said, to 1 John. Yet the growing number of attempts to determine their historical setting, and the very fact of their inclusion within the canon, invites at least some consideration of their response to that setting and of their theological contribution to that canon. It may be that we can only really describe the questions the two letters pose, and not the answers.

Church and ministry

The Second Epistle is addressed to a, perhaps 'the', church and is concerned with its boundaries – who may be allowed in; 3 John reflects a dispute about authority and again about permitted membership. Thus church and ministry are implicitly or explicitly, a concern for both letters. Starting from the author's own position, the significance of his self-designation as 'the Elder' remains unsolved, yet it has often been held to reflect a particular understanding of ministry which may be under attack in the events behind 3 John.[106] Our earlier discussion of the situation behind 3 John (pp. 8–11) showed that attempts to identify the title with specific authority structures or with known groups in the early church have been largely unsuccessful. Here of course 1 John offers little help, for ministry is one theme we have found no occasion to discuss except in the negative sense that the author's authority there is rooted in witness and is not exclusive to a limited group defined by any form of appointment (pp. 23–6). Such an undefined

---

[106] See above, 'introduction', pp. 8–9 and Lieu, *Second and Third Epistles*, 52–64.

authority might well contribute to the conflict that has now emerged, but it must be said that there is nothing in the letters themselves or specifically in the epithet 'Elder' to suggest such an authority is being defended. The title itself is ambiguous, and the letters do little more than suggest that the author feels able to write authoritatively from one church to another and equally feels himself responsible for and implicated in the reception given to the 'travelling brethren'.

In opposition to the Elder in 3 John stands Diotrephes, who is condemned for his refusal to receive either the Elder (or his letter) or some travelling 'brethren', and for his 'love of first place'. Some have argued that Diotrephes represents just that form of structured, local authority that we have not found in 1 John – an embryonic monarchical bishop; according to this reading the Elder stands for and defends an authority which was limited neither by geography nor by appointment, but was grounded in something tied to the individual, perhaps the witness he bore or the tradition to which he was bound, or it might be his sense of call or the (spiritual) gifts he displayed.[107] That such a tension between 'institutional' and 'charismatic' should be found within the New Testament has proved attractive to many interpreters in recent years, but, as I have intimated, there is nothing in the title 'Elder' or in the letters to align their author with a particular 'non-institutional', and even less a charismatic, style of ministry. The most we might note is that 'loving first place' is similar in form to other words such as 'loving honour' which in Graeco-Roman city life were epithets of honour – this was a proper ambition; the Elder reverses such values, but not necessarily against a growing 'establishment' in the church. A connection with the Johannine 'openness' about ministry is probable, but it may be that the author's failure to engage in any debate about the nature or source of his own or of his opponent's authority is the most significant aspect of the issue; we have a war of words and of name-calling, not a theological debate.[108]

Linked with this, it is often noted that 3 John alone uses the

---

[107] For further discussion see Lieu, *Second and Third Epistles*, 150–4.
[108] *Ibid.*, 156–9.

word *ekklesia*, 'church' (9,10),[109] although it is easier to comment on the silence of the rest of the Johannine tradition than on its presence here. Yet it remains true that, despite its brevity, 3 John uses a number of 'institutional' terms not found elsewhere in the Johannine writings but more characteristic of the Pauline tradition, particularly in missionary contexts: 'to send forward', 'worthily of God' (6), 'to help' and 'fellow-workers' (8); it may be reading too much into so brief a passage (6–8), but this does suggest a more open attitude to missionary activity than we detected in 1 John. Yet 3 John offers no other justification than that these brethren have 'gone out for the sake of the name' – which is more likely to be a reference to God than to Jesus, who is not otherwise mentioned in this letter.

The Second Epistle also presupposes a gathered community; as we have seen, it remains most probable that the 'elect lady' of the address (1,5 and the elect sister of 13) represents a church rather than a particular individual with her children. Does this largely unparalleled form of address point to a particular understanding of the church? Certainly it is hard to find any purely historical reason for this 'cover' – there is no sense that persecution is necessitating code names. There are Jewish precedents where Jerusalem appears as a mother (Isa. 54; Baruch 4–5) and the image is one that continues in early Christian thought (Gal. 4:21f.; 2 Cor. 11:2 and see especially 1 Pet. 5:13, probably of the church in Rome). The epithet 'elect' is not a Johannine term, but it too belongs to the language of Israel and so can be used of Christians as God's elect people (1 Pet. 2:9; Isa. 43:20); in early Christian writings it is used more in the plural of all Christians than in the singular, and sometimes has special force in eschatological contexts of those whose ultimate salvation is assured (Mark 13:20,22,27). All this might suggest a sharper sense of the nature and calling of the church, viewed as more than the community of those who believe, than we would have expected from 1 John. Certainly the sense of assurance is sustained in the greeting with its

[109] Schweizer, *Church Order*, 12c, p. 128, sees it as the term reserved for the opposing faction 'whom the monarchical bishop would like to subject to himself'. However, the Elder sees no problem in using it himself.

affirmative 'Grace . . . *shall be* with us' in place of the implied wish ('may grace . . . be') of the Pauline greetings on which this has been modelled.

Both letters envisage exclusion from the church: in 3 John it is resented as unmerited rather than wrong in principle (10); in 2 John refusal of welcome is enjoined against both those who 'do not bear this teaching' (10) and, by implication, those who ignore this injunction (11, as has happened in 3 John 10). We might expect this to reflect an understanding of the church as not so much a school for sinners as the refuge of the elect; it is easy to draw parallels to show that it is groups which have the strongest sense of their calling and of the hostility or 'lostness' of all others which are most likely to exercise the sharpest discipline against straying members. They operate with 'high' boundaries and must make clear to those within as well as those without the chasm which separates them. This would not be inconsistent with the impression gained from 1 John of the community's self-understanding, but the brevity and allusiveness of both letters make it difficult to determine the motivating forces behind the action.

Tradition and teaching

The concern with teaching in 2 John introduces a term not found in the First Epistle, which prefers the more dynamic language of 'what you have heard'. Here what is called for is 'abiding in the teaching' (9); although 'abiding' is a theme characteristic of 1 John (pp. 41–5), for its location to be 'the teaching' rather than God or Christ brings us closer to exhortations to faithfulness to the tradition found in the later writings of the New Testament (1 Tim. 2:15; 2 Tim. 3:14). The content of this teaching is not specified, but within the structure of the letter it seems to be encapsulated in the love command (4–6) and the right understanding of Jesus (7) which precede the exhortation. The former is familiar from 1 John (see p. 55), although here there is no suggestion that it is also new – it is enough that it belongs to that 'which we have had from the beginning'; the latter is more problematic.

As in 1 John it is introduced against the background of the advent of false prophets who carry false teaching. Here that false teaching is specified as their failure to confess 'Jesus Christ as the "one coming" in flesh'. It may be that the concern is identical with that of 1 John 4:1ff. (see pp. 75–8). However, the verb here translated 'the one coming' is not a past tense as in 1 John 4 but a present (which could also be read as a future). It is just possible that the reference is to the expected coming (or parousia) of Jesus which is here asserted to be 'in flesh'.[110] It seems more probable that the language is being used loosely, dependent on the confession in 1 John but combining it with the description of Jesus within the Gospel tradition as 'the coming one' (John 3:31). If this is so the letter adds nothing to the Johannine understanding of Jesus and his ministry; instead this together with the command acts as a. pointer to the traditional language of the community.

A recurring theme in these two Epistles is 'the truth', particularly in the phrase 'in (the) truth' (six out of eleven occurrences of the term). The word is both a favourite within the Johannine tradition and notoriously difficult to interpret systematically. In the First Epistle it belongs to the dualist pattern of thought, being used regularly in contrast to falsehood (1:6,8; 2:4,21; 4:6). This is not so here – and the language of falsehood is nowhere used despite the polemic in which the letters are engaged; the deceivers are not called 'false prophets' in 2 John, which, if the letter is dependent on 1 John, may be deliberate. It has been argued that 'truth' in 2 and 3 John is coming close to the idea of 'the true teaching' or the 'faith' of the Pastoral Epistles;[111] this is probably to give it too great precision. Certainly 'truth' belongs to the community and to its members (2 John 1–2), but the repeated 'in truth' (1,3; 3 John 1) seems to have little more content than a slogan; many

---

110 A number of older commentaries accept this, including C. Gore, *The Epistles of St. John* (London, 1920), 226 and Westcott, *Epistles*, 218: 'the thought centres upon the present perfection of the Lord's Manhood which *is* still, and is to be manifested'; it has recently been revived by G. Strecker, 'Die Anfänge der johanneischen Schule', *NTS* 32 (1986), 31–47, 35.

111 So R. Bergmeier, 'Zum Verfasserproblem des II und III Johannesbriefes', *ZNW* 57 (1966), 93–100.

readers may have seen in it no more than the conventional 'sincerely' of contemporary letters. Equally, the concern with walking 'in truth' (2 John 4; 3 John 3) probably does mean more than 'behaving honestly' – thus in 3 John 3 it also says 'walking in *the* truth' – yet it is not easy to specify the content of the image beyond perhaps 'living according to the principles of Johannine Christianity'. A stronger note may be sounded in v. 12, where witness is borne 'by the truth itself'. This could suggest a personification of truth or even identification of truth with Christ; yet this idiom too is found in secular contexts and may have been read as little more than conventional. The concern with the term 'truth' is not matched by a substantial contribution to its Johannine significance, and this failure may not be a reflection only of the occasional nature of the letters but of a shift in theological understanding towards a tendency to catchwords.

A new theme comes in the exhortation to Gauis to imitate not evil but good (3 John 11). As a basis for ethical action imitation of other Christians has other new Testament parallels, although not in the Johannine tradition (1 Cor. 4:16; 11:1; 1 Thess. 1:6; 2:14; 2 Thess. 3:7). Here the model is not (as often) Christ or the author, but Demetrius (12), who, as just noted, is described in terms reminiscent of the approbation given to figures in authority in both Christian and non-Christian sources.[112] The bland statement that 'the one who does good is of God' (11) could, out of context, be given a universal reference – that ultimately it is acts of charity which determine a person's standing before God (rather than acceptance or rejection of Jesus).[113] Attractive though some will find this, in context the reference is surely limited to the contrasting behaviour of Diotrephes and Demetrius. The phrase 'is of God' is Johannine (above, pp. 39–41), and so perhaps is 'has (not) seen God', which cannot then be pressed for the question whether or not humankind can see God and live (see John 1:18; 6:46; 1 John 4:12,20).

---

[112] Lieu, *Second and Third Epistles*, 118–20.
[113] So T. Horvath, '3 Jn 11b. An Early Ecumenical Creed?', *ExpTim* 85 (1973), 339–40.

The harvest gleaned is meagre, but perhaps some may feel that it is already more abundant than these two letters can yield. The argument here is that, while we must recognise the occasional nature of the texts, and our total ignorance of what else the author would have said given space and time, they do reflect theological views both in their expression and in the events which provoked them. The task is both to respect their specificity and to sketch those views as far as possible. It may be, however, that the theological task they prompt is a different one, namely to ask how to understand their very place within the New Testament and within the Johannine corpus, a question to which we must turn next.

CHAPTER 3

The Epistles within the Johannine tradition and the New Testament

Within the richness of the New Testament the Johannine writings maintain a distinctive and honoured place. Shared idiosyncrasies of language and thought bind the Gospel and Epistles of John together; despite a fundamentally different perspective and apparent background, the Apocalypse too seems to have established links with this tradition. While Johannine theology has long been recognised as sounding a major voice within the New Testament, its historical place within the development of the early church has been vigorously disputed. The traditional identification of the author of all the Johannine writings as John the Apostle and son of Zebedee located them in close connection with the ministry of Jesus and within the apostolic church. The surrender of that identification has often gone hand in hand with a supposition that Johannine thought represents an isolated and marginal form of first-century Christianity, only really coming into its own after the middle of the second century. This rests on the apparent lack of earlier attestation of the Gospel, on its supposed earlier popularity among gnostic groups, and on the limited contacts between the Johannine and other writings of the New Testament.[1]

The other side of this is the sharply defined common identity of the Johannine writings (with the probable exception of Revelation, which has its own idiosyncrasies). Even if, or rather especially if, they are not by the same author, the fact

---

[1] See D. M. Smith, 'Johannine Christianity: Some Reflections on its Character and Delineation', *NTS* 21 (1976), 222–48, reprinted in *Johannine Christianity* (Edinburgh, 1987), 1–36, esp. 4–9.

that they share language, style, terminology and patterns of theological thought and outlook points to a tradition which was encapsulated within a defined group. It is this which makes it possible to talk about Johannine theology and also about Johannine Christianity.

One response to this state of affairs is to read 1 John in the light of the Gospel on the assumption of common thought if not common authorship, and so to create a unitary, often thematic, theology. This need not reduce 1 John to the position of a footnote or supporting voice so much as contributing a chapter whose true significance is only seen in the light of the whole work. Such an interpretation, which particularly suits common Johannine themes like 'love', gives a depth and texture to 1 John which it does not have when read on its own; yet it may also lead to a loosing of the historical particularity and therefore of the theological particularity of the Epistle.[2] While recognising the insights and richness of this approach, I think it is better to start from the letters' original intention and inner distinctiveness. The Gospel and Epistles are not, together or individually, monochrome; the tradition they represent was a growing one, expressed in different responses to different situations (see my introduction, pp. 17–20 above). They also represent different types of literature; the Gospel invites being set alongside the other Gospels, the Epistles alongside the other letters and pastoral writings of the church. So we can ask about the Epistles' place within and contribution to both Johannine theology and the theology of the New Testament.

THE JOHANNINE TRADITION

As has been pointed out more than once, the Johannine tradition represented at least by the Epistles and Gospel is characterised by a 'family likeness' which even extends to

---

[2] We have seen this in the studies of Feuillet, *Le Mystère de l'amour*, and Vellanickal, *Divine Sonship*. It is also done less systematically when the Gospel is used to interpret the ambiguities or silences of 1 John as by Burge, *Anointed Community*, who thus finds a far richer understanding of the spirit in 1 John than I have done.

matters of style and grammatical construction; a number of commentaries give lists of words and phrases common to the Gospel and First Epistle, many of which are hardly to be found elsewhere in the New Testament. The common matter extends to what we might call the theological world view as well as to the terms in which it is expressed. Both speak of the world in negative terms, of being 'of the world', and of its hatred for both Jesus and his followers. Both speak of the new commandment of love for one another, of Jesus laying down his life, of abiding in 'him' or Jesus, of 'we' who have seen and born witness. Both speak of salvation in terms of knowledge and of eternal life, and see this salvation in largely present or realised terms; both stress Jesus as Son of God. So we could continue – as A. E. Brooke says, 'To quote all [the similarities] that exist would involve printing practically the whole of the Epistle and a large part of the Gospel.'[3] Allowing for their brevity, many of these are to be found in the smaller Epistles, although 3 John has a surprising number of new terms and concepts.[4]

Even within these similarities there are differences. It is often noted that 1 John uses against internal enemies language which in the Gospel is used of those outside, chiefly the Jews.[5] While both writings adopt a dualism of light and darkness, life and death, love and hatred, truth and falsehood, in each case the dualism is more marked in the Epistle than in the Gospel – as is seen when the relative frequency of the negative as opposed to the positive terms is noted. Thus the Gospel uses 'truth' 25 times and 'falsehood' words only 3 times, and 1 John 9 and 8 respectively; John uses 'light' 22 times and 'darkness' 9, and 1 John 6 and 7 respectively. This distinction is ignored by Bultmann when he draws extensively from 1 John to elaborate Johannine dualism, but elsewhere tends to use the Gospel to speak of what is 'Johannine'.[6]

As has been equally amply stated, the Epistles also exhibit a

---

[3] Brooke, *Epistles*, ix.
[4] Particularly terms which may be described as ecclesiastical, missionary and ethical, such as 'church', 'send forward', 'fellow-worker', 'gentile', 'stranger', 'receive', 'do good/evil' etc.; see Lieu, *Second and Third Epistles*, 218–19.
[5] Such as being of the devil (John 8:44; 1 John 3:8); so Brown, *Epistles*, 92–3.
[6] R. Bultmann, *Theology of the New Testament*, 2 vols. (London, 1952, 1955), II, 15–20.

number of differences from the Gospel in style, language and
thought. These, as well as the distinct settings implied by the
documents, have prompted the debate about common authorship and led to the now majority position that different authors
are responsible for at least the Gospel and Epistles. A number
of these differences have emerged during the course of our
discussion of the theology of the Epistles; so too has the way
apparently similar material is used in distinct ways. It is this
which has prompted the position taken here that rather than
one being dependent on the other, the Gospel and Epistle
independently work from a common body of Johannine tradition. This means that the Epistle's contribution was not in
intention to correct any misunderstanding that had arisen or
might arise from the Gospel.[7] In what follows the differences as
often noted do provide a starting point for exploring the
Epistles' role within the Johannine tradition, but there is no
full discussion of those aspects of the Gospel's thought which
are absent from the Epistles; such discussions are to be found
elsewhere and would entail longer analysis of the Gospel than
space permits.[8] Instead the clear concerns of the letters add
their own voice to a Johannine theology.

The importance of Jesus

The absence of any real interest in the life of Jesus, including
his resurrection, sits oddly with the emphasis on belief that he
is the Christ or Son of God. It is often said that for John it is
'belief *in* Jesus' (commitment) which is important, while for 1
John, prompted by a new situation, it is 'belief *that*' (belief
about). This is only partly true; the Gospel too has key
characters confess who Jesus is (John 6:69; 11:27; 20:28), gives
Jesus the great 'I am' claims, and centres much of the debate
with the Jews on who Jesus is and what support he has for his
claims. Yet for 1 John far more than for the Gospel the

---

[7] For this as a common approach to 1 John see my introduction, p. 15.
[8] For a list of words and phrases in the Gospel not found in 1 John see Brooke, *Epistles*,
   xii; on specific themes see Lieu, *Second and Third Epistles*, 188, 221 and for a general
   discussion of the difference of focus between Gospel and First Epistle, 205–6.

emphasis lies to a greater extent in maintaining a confession (with its overtones of public acknowledgement) than in the moment of decision. Whether or not in the same external context, both Gospel and Epistle treat as central the affirmation that Jesus is the Son of God and take this beyond what it might mean in a Jewish 'messianic' setting (see above, pp. 71–2); 1 John's particular emphasis is to deny the possibility of any genuine relationship with God where this confession of Jesus is absent. Despite our caution about an overly polemical reading of 1 John, it does seem that the letter is prompted in this denial by those who claimed some 'Christian' status yet whose 'confessional' status is perceived as inadequate, an issue which if present in the Gospel (as perhaps in 6:66–71) is far more oblique. For 1 John what is believed about Jesus is of inalterable importance, although we have found it difficult to discover any detailed content behind that firm assertion. The reality of his humanity and participation in human experience may be at issue, although poorly articulated even in 4:2. Here it is possible to contrast the Gospel's openness to a reading which sees only Jesus' divinity, his unity with God (John 10:30), freedom from the agony of Gethsemane, foreknowledge and readiness to speak of his origin from and home with God the Father. Some have seen this contrast as a causal relationship: the Gospel's picture was developed in an even more 'docetic' direction by the 'heretics' of 1 John, thus necessitating the letter's restatement of the humanity of Jesus.[9] However, I have argued that the main thrust of 1 John's thought is not anti-docetic and should not be so related to the Gospel.

What is important for 1 John is Jesus' significance for forgiveness and deliverance from sin. It is often suggested that the images 1 John uses are more 'primitive' than those of the Gospel, calling upon sacrificial ideas from the Temple cult, blood and propitiation (1:7; 2:2; 4:10; above, pp. 63–4); for John Jesus' death is the focal point of his lifting up or glorification, and sin is more to do with the unbelief with which Jesus is met. While this may be an over-simplification (see

[9] See above p. 18, n. 24.

John 1:29), 1 John does wrestle with sin as a continuing problem – something to which we shall return as we look at its place within the NT – and also presents Jesus as continuing to act for his people both in dealing with sin and as a pattern to be followed (see above, pp. 73–5). At the same time he makes clear that any such 'sacrificial' models do not introduce a tension between Father and Son, for forgiveness is equally rooted in the character of the Father (1:9). This must be set alongside the Gospel's presentation of Jesus as bringer of salvation (expressed through a rich variety of images not found in 1 John) and as the one who reveals and provides a way to the Father.

Despite the absence of the last theme, 1 John is notable for its theocentricity. We have seen (pp. 78–9) how many of the images which in John are focussed on Jesus here have God as their centre (abiding, knowing). While the necessity of right belief about Jesus is stressed, it is God who is the centre of religious experience, God who is light and love, God who is the source of both the commandments and of the believer's begetting. It is perhaps inevitable that the Gospel, telling the story of Jesus, should put Jesus in the centre, albeit as the way to God; 1 John's sense of Jesus' continuing presence in the lives of believers may be less developed than that of the Gospel, but his sense of the immediacy of the relationship with God is very strong and rich in the imagery used.

The life and experience of the community

Undoubtedly the Fourth Gospel presupposes a community of Christians with a defined sense of identity, an identity which has often been explored through the language and method of the Gospel. The picture drawn, most vividly by W. Meeks and adopted by many others,[10] is of a 'sectarian' group with a sharp sense of their calling or election and of the chasm that separated them, to whom belong light and life, from those outside. In the Gospel that sense is mediated through the

[10] W. A. Meeks, 'The Man from Heaven in Johannine Sectarianism', *JBL* 91 (1972), 44–72.

telling of the story of Jesus, while the community are invisible other than as represented by the disciples; in 1 John the community are much more visible as the recipients of the author's concerns. As a community their sense of corporate identity goes hand in hand with an individualism expressed through the metaphors of religious experience – being born, abiding, knowing. Sometimes, as in to whom the spirit is given (p. 47 above), it is not clear whether we are to think of the individual or group. The realised eschatology and language of religious experience, characteristic of both Gospel and Epistle, could lead to a community which was made up of individuals whose primary concern was their own personal election. This is countered in 1 John by the repeated emphasis on the command to love one another, which is both given a specific application (3:17; cf. 5:16) and also set against the disruption caused by those who had left the community. This apparently more practical ('ethical') use of the distinctive Johannine love command is different from that of the Gospel, where it belongs to a reciprocal complex of love between Father, Son and disciples and so becomes an expression of their essential unity.[11] Yet it must be admitted that the reaction against those who had left, labelling them as 'antichrists' and aligning them with the 'world', itself set over against God, reflects the less happy consequences of this Johannine self-identity. In 2 John we see a more overt expression of this in the explicit refusal of hospitality and even a greeting, perhaps representing a stage further in the self-protective sense of community. As with the problem over sin committed by believers, the response reveals the difficulty an emphasis on present possession of salvation has with actual failure or falling away. The other side of the coin may be the largely negative view of the world, perhaps suggesting little enthusiasm for positive mission and little trust in the success of others (4:4–6). However, 3 John with its distinctive vocabulary

---

[11] This difference is stressed by M. Lattke, *Einheit im Wort*, SANT 41 (Munich, 1975), 106, but whereas he suggests that in 1 John love is ethically understood, I have argued that here too it is an expression of unity but on a different basis from the Gospel (p. 70 above).

seems to adopt a more positive view to mission and suggests a more varied approach with Johannine theology than has survived in the main letter.[12]

It has sometimes been supposed that the schism which split the community of 1 John owed a great deal to a one-sided confidence in the present possession of the spirit, justifying new teachings and patterns of behaviour, a confidence inspired by the high value given the spirit-paraclete in the Gospel (see above, pp. 29, 46–9). There is little in the Epistle to support this, and the letter's relative silence regarding the spirit must be taken as a 'thin' area in its theology and not as deliberate avoidance of a theme the 'enemy' had taken from the Gospel and made their own. Yet it is true that 1 John does hold up against the threat posed 'that which they have heard from the beginning'. We may contrast this with the balance proposed by the Gospel where the spirit both leads them in all truth and yet proclaims only what it has received from Jesus (John 16:13–14); this does not mean that 1 John has lost what the Gospel achieved and, in giving tradition priority over creativity, marks a step (?decline) into early catholicism.[13] This charge may be truer of 2 and 3 John, which express a related concern through their use of 'truth'; in 2 John at least it does seem that brief apothegms (5–6; 7) express 'the teaching' (9) largely through echoing the words of an earlier document (1 John). Certainly here the potential rigidity of Johannine thought about faithfulness with the past has won out against creativity. Yet if we are to speak of tradition in 1 John, it is something heard and proclaimed, something that dwells within the believer and becomes part of her or his relationship with God. For all its importance, its actual expressed content is surprisingly meagre, neither is there any interest in the process of transmission or present authentication. Instead it is some-

---

12 See above, p. 93; the Gospel's understanding of mission is often undervalued, as is perceptively and well argued by T. Okure, *The Johannine Approach to Mission*, WUNT 31 (Tübingen, 1988).

13 Thus H. Conzelmann is often quoted for his description of 1 John as a 'Johannine Pastoral' ('Was von Anfang war', in *Neutestamentliche Studien für R. Bultmann*, ed. W. Eltester, BZNW 21 (Berlin, 1954), 194–201); even Burge, *Anointed Community*, 219–21, who rejects any suggestion that in the Epistle we have a budding 'early catholicism', does say that the 'conservative, preserving emphasis has won out.'

thing incumbent on the individual but also belonging to the community. It is this balance between the call to abide by what they have heard from the beginning and a confidence in the individual's possession of the truth as a member of the community which marks 1 John's distinctive response to a common question within the Johannine tradition.

Love and faith

If there is a single theme in 1 John, it is that claims to religious experience or status have no validity if they remain independent of life as it is lived. Love of God and love of a brother are so inseparable that one becomes the test or proof of the other. Walking in the light is both a moral category and a religious one. It is not just a case of external test and internal reality; as we have seen, the boundary between the two can become dissolved. It is true that the 'ethical' dimension is very unspecific and that behaviour seems primarily directed towards other members of the community; there is no consideration of how they are to behave 'in the world'. Yet this is characteristic of the whole of the Johannine tradition; the Gospel is devoid of the moral teaching found elsewhere in the Jesus tradition, for example in Jesus' teaching on divorce or in the Sermon on the Mount. Even the love command in the Gospel has more to do with sharing in the divine unity than with practical behaviour (see above, pp. 68–9). John mainly identifies sin with unbelief and affirms that the one who believes does not come to judgement (3:18); for him acceptance of Jesus as the Son sent by the Father is literally a life and death decision. Those who do so believe have passed through judgement and can be said to have entered into the fullness traditionally associated with the future age – life, unity with God, light. The Gospel certainly knows of apostasy and betrayal by those who had seemed to have taken that step (6:66–71); his response is to affirm that preservation in salvation lies in God's choice and protection and that unity can only be grounded in remaining within the divine unity of love (17). The response of 1 John is to face the members of the community directly with an unavoidable imperative. The decision for faith is a decision for a community, a decision to be worked out in the life of the community.[14] Whether or not we decide he is successful, what is at once a tension and a unity between the statement of assurance and the demand or imperative, and between the relationship with God and its practical outworking in corporate life, is complementary to the Gospel's theological insights.

THE NEW TESTAMENT

The distinctive style of the Johannine tradition means it has a major contribution to give to NT theology, a contribution in which 1 John shares. In particular it affirms the 'already' of Christian existence over against the 'not yet' of future hope. This is a tension found throughout the New Testament; the early church were united in seeing in Jesus, in his preaching of the kingdom and in his resurrection, the inbreaking of the new age. With equal confidence they looked forward to the full accomplishment of that age. Different NT writers express the tension of the interim in different ways, and put varying emphasis on what is yet to come. Future hope is certainly not lacking in the Johannine tradition, either in the Gospel (5:28–9; 6:39; 12:48; 17:26) or Epistles (1 John 2:28–3:2; 4:17; 2 John 8), but the greatest weight is on the present possession of the blessings of the new age, on eternal life as already experienced (1 John 3:14). The two aspects are not well integrated in the Gospel, with the result that the elements of future hope have often been assigned to a later redactor.[15] Although the train of thought is not fully clear, we have seen how 1 John seeks to root the future hope in the absolute confidence of the present so that the completeness of the present is barely compromised.[16]

14 In Lieu, *Second and Third Epistles*, 206, I have argued that whereas in the Gospel it is Jesus who plays the focal role, in 1 John it is the community: thus in John 15:33 Jesus has conquered the world, while in 1 John 5:4, 5; 4:4 the victory is won by 'you' or 'our faith'.

15 A view most commonly associated with Bultmann (see *Theology* II, 39) although followed by others.

16 So we have rejected the common assertion that 1 John marks a return to a more primitive eschatology than that of the Gospel; see above, pp. 88–90.

The already/not yet tension in early Christian thought inevitably led to problems when the actual behaviour of converts was being faced. Paul had to encourage his churches to display in their lives what they were 'in Christ' – become what you are! (See Rom. 6:11–12). Hebrews struggles with those who once enlightened then fall away (Heb. 6:4–6), and led the way for future debate over postbaptismal sin (see above, pp. 59–64). Inevitably the problem is greatest where there is the strongest sense of having already entered into the new age or where the final battle lines are drawn up. This is the context for 1 John's own attempt to grapple with the problem of sin. We have seen that the unresolved tension in his answer is the product of the two settings in which sin is placed. Firstly, within a sharply dualistic scheme, it belongs to the sphere opposed to God, the sphere over which Jesus won a decisive victory; yet it is also a reality of human life, to deny whose existence is to deny the basis on which all people, including believers, stand before God. The author of 1 John joins the majority of NT writers in affirming that in his life and death Jesus dealt with sin completely – once and for all (Rom. 3:25; 1 Pet. 3:18; Heb. 10:12; 1 John 3:5); yet he offers a way forward for the dilemma posed by continuing sin by presenting Jesus as continuing to act on behalf of those who ought not to but who do sin, and who confess their sins. Further, in separating out that sin which leads to death, probably apostasy, and encouraging intercessory prayer on behalf of a fellow believer who falls into some other form of sin, he sets the problem within the mutual responsibility of the community.

Elsewhere in the NT, particularly in the letters of Paul, we find a sustained effort to work out the consequences for practical issues in the lives of believers, of existence between the now and not yet. This is not 1 John's concern, except for the demand for mutal love – and even here we must look elsewhere to see how this works in practice (Rom. 13:8–10; Gal. 5:13–15). Yet 1 John reiterates more forcefully than any other NT writer the unity between the relationship with God and relationships with others, and in expressing this in terms of love grounds it all in the context of the initiating love of God (1 John 4:19–20).

Moreover, he does this not so much by argument and logical clarity as by the style and form of what he has written. As we have seen, the approach taken by 1 John does not need to face the polarity between 'faith and works' as means to salvation; he sees only the inner and outer expressions of a relationship with God as a single whole, as present in their completeness or not present at all. However, there is no hint as to how this found practical application in the Johannine tradition; presumably patterns of life in society had to be developed and issues such as those we meet in the Pauline Epistles answered, but there is no suggestion as to how those answers might be developed.

One aspect of this is the question of authority within the community. Johannine Christianity has often been seen as representing a counter-balance to the developing awareness of church structures and ministry elsewhere in the NT.[17] Like the Gospel, 1 John has little of the technical language of the church (although some surfaces in 3 John) but certainly does reflect a community or communities with a distinctive self-awareness. We have seen that even the authority claimed by the author is based not on any personal qualifications of calling or person such as characterise the opening of other NT letters but on the anonymous authority of witness, which is also shared with all believers. Although addressed as 'children', members of the community are not immature and in need of nurturing (as in 1 Cor. 3:1; Heb. 5:11–12); all have equal access to knowledge and to the truth, and an equal hold on 'that which was from the beginning'. Another facet of this is of course the 'realised eschatology' which stresses both the assurance of their election and the fullness of their present experience; another may be the absence of any indication of whence they have come, whether they are of Jewish or Gentile background or include both groups. The other NT letters may offer us more of the varied circumstances and characters of the first Christian groups; 1

---

[17] See above, p. 92 on 3 John, and generally H. v. Campenhausen, *Ecclesiastical Authority and Spiritual Power in the Church of the First Three Centuries* (London, 1969), 121–3, 136–41, who speaks of 'the free spirituality of the Johannine world, with its horror of all hierarchical organisation and its intense confidence in the power of the "truth"' (136).

John focusses on what they are as those who believe and rests their corporate authority in that.

We have dismissed suggestion that either the community as perceived by 1 John, or key figures within it, are spirit-marked, so that in 3 John we see the conflict between charism and institution.[18] On the other hand 1 John's concern with 'tradition' has earned it the label 'the Johannine Pastoral', while others would argue that it is 2 and 3 John with their emphasis on 'truth' which represent this development.[19] Do these Epistles represent early hints of 'early catholicism' within the NT? Those who so argue would point to the authority given to an apparently static 'tradition' and its transmission, to faith as confession and right belief, to the development of ecclesial machinery for dealing with sin (confession and prayer by other members of the community), and to the categorising of sins as mortal or otherwise. If not in 1 John then in 2 John we find the development of a discipline which includes a form of excommunication, and this is but an expression of the understanding of the church (even if not so called) as the only locus of both election and salvation. Yet it would be wrong to label 1 John as representing early catholicism or even to see these traits as evidence of its date towards the end of the NT period. Faith, tradition or ecclesiastical structures are never objectified; what is more striking is the absence of the defences erected against false belief in the Pastoral Epistles, where transmission of tradition and authority are important, and detailed patterns of behaviour and organisation are set out. We come back to the central place given to the community and to the unity of their experience and tradition. The problems and the potential of that response as a contribution to the NT only become clear when the Johannine tradition is viewed as a whole, including as it does both the collapse into slogans in 2 and 3 John and the razor's edge profundity of the Gospel.

[18] So Campenhausen, *Ecclesiastical Authority*, 122; see above, p. 92.
[19] See above, n. 12; Bultmann, *Epistles*, 1, finds early catholicism in 2 John. The arguments for early catholicism in these Epistles are assessed by C. Clifton Black, 'The Johannine Epistles and the Question of Early Catholicism', *NovT* 28 (1986), 131–58, with the conclusion that the criteria for recognising early catholicism are inadequate.

CHAPTER 4

The significance of the Johannine Epistles in the church

THE EPISTLES IN THE CHURCH

While modern study tends to focus on the message of the Epistles in their original setting, their place within the New Testament canon both reflects and in the past has prompted a more general or 'catholic' understanding. All three Epistles are included among the seven 'catholic' Epistles (with 1 and 2 Peter, James and Jude), which were deemed to have a general or universal reference for the church compared with the letters of Paul, addressed as they were to specific situations and issues. The epithet 'catholic' was applied to 1 John as early as the middle of the third century and perhaps earlier still, and may only then have been extended to the other six.[1] Certainly 1 John was readily accepted by the wider church; even in the East, where there was considerably more disagreement about the catholic Epistles, 1 John together with 1 Peter seems to have been widely acknowledged.[2] By contrast 2 and 3 John took much longer to achieve a secure place in the canon; few of the early Christian writers quote or refer to them, and some explicitly exclude them; their authorship by the 'Elder' continued to provoke debate and some found their specific address, particularly that of 2 John to a woman, inappropriate for 'catholic' Epistles! Inevitably their brevity and 3 John's

---

[1] The term is used of 1 John by Dionysius of Alexandria in Eusebius, *Church History* VII.25.7 and possibly (although this is less likely) even earlier in the Muratorian canon at the end of the second century. A. Jülicher, *Einleitung in das Neue Testament* (Tübingen, 1931), 186–7 argues that the term was applied first to 1 John, perhaps in contrast to 2 and 3 John.

[2] On this and what follows see Lieu, *Second and Third Epistles*, 5–36.

lack of doctrinal content contributed little to their defence, and
so finally it must have been their antiquity, and their association with the First Epistle and thus with the Gospel which
offered support to their supposed authorship by the apostle
John and ensured their place within the New Testament. Small
wonder, however, that in the Middle Ages some explicitly
accorded 2 and 3 John less authority than 1 John while
affirming the importance of the main letter as a resource for
doctrine. Modern historical interest in their place in the
development of the early church has to some extent rehabili-
tated 2 and 3 John as worthy of interest and interpretation;
however, since this has meant acknowledging their specific
setting and purpose, they can no longer be called 'catholic'
in the original sense but perhaps only in the loose sense
adopted by S. Smalley for all three, that the message they
expressed 'subsequently proved indispensable for the life and
survival of the church universal'.[3]

It is therefore chiefly 1 John which has made its contribution
to the development of the church's thought. The only real
exception to this is the use of 2 John 9–11 to sanction the
exclusion from fellowship of a variety of heretics or schismatics
from gnostics to Arians, contributing on the way to the debate
whether rebaptism was to be administered to those who sought
readmission to the church.[4] While much is to be learned from
these Epistles' emphasis on right belief, our recognition of the
particular circumstances of the Johannine community and of
the theology which has provoked this response will probably
make us less inclined to remove these verses from context and
apply their refusal of even so much as a greeting to all who 'do
not teach our doctrine'!

At various times in the history of the church this emphasis
on right belief and on the right behaviour which must accom-

---

[3] Smalley, *1, 2, 3 John*, xxxiv. B. S. Childs, *The New Testament as Canon: An Introduction*
(London, 1984), 486–7 seeks to retain a 'universal' understanding of the Epistles
because this is the context in which they were preserved within the canon. In his
concern for the continuing function of Scripture within the church he probably
undervalues the insights offered by fully recognising the historical circumstances of
the letters.

[4] See Lieu, *Second and Third Epistles*, 30–4.

pany it has been evoked on the authority of 1 John. This theme as well as the insights into religious experience and the language of religious experience have made 1 John a perennial source of comment and reflection; affirmations such as 'God is love' have been taken from their setting and become a foundation stone in the Christian understanding of God. On the negative side the label 'antichrist' has been taken from its specific reference in 1 and 2 John and joined with other epithets (for example 'son of perdition': John 17:12; 2 Thess. 2:3) to characterise a range of 'opponents' of the church from the soon-to-return Nero to the Pope in the Westminster Confession.

More specifically, the distinction between those sins for which the readers are urged to intercede and the 'sin unto death' (1 John 5:16–17) has contributed to the development of the doctrine of sin, in particular to a separation between types of sins and the possibilities of forgiveness. Tertullian appeals to these verses to establish that there are some sins for which there is no pardon – murder, idolatry, injustice, apostasy, adultery and fornication (*de Pud.* 2.14–16; 19.26–8); in the medieval period the distinction made was between mortal and venial sins – for the former confession is needed, for the latter only the private prayer for forgiveness.[5] Whatever the need in any system of moral teaching for a distinction between sins, the appeal to 1 John 5:16 to construct such a division is contradicted by the letter's original intention; this, as we have seen, was surely to highlight apostasy, understood and experienced within the community as the conscious rejection of a faith once held, that is as a rejection of life itself.

One contribution of 1 John to the theology of the church which we have nowhere discussed is the so-called Johannine 'Comma', the words familiar to readers of the Authorised Version at 1 John 5:7–8, 'Because there are three that bear record *in heaven, the Father, the Word and the Holy Ghost: and these three are one. And three that bear witness in earth*, the spirit, and the water, and the blood: and these three agree in one'. The presence of so explicit a trinitarian witness within the New

---

[5] A full discussion is given in Westcott, *Epistles*, 199–204.

Testament would be both surprising and important. However, despite having been enthusiastically defended in the past, more because of their dogmatic than their text-critical importance, it is evident that these words were not penned by the author of 1 John but came into the text as a gloss, invited by the theme of three in unity. Only a few, very late, Greek manuscripts contain them, and the evidence suggests that they originated in the third century within the Latin tradition, only really entered the tradition of Greek New Testament editions in the sixteenth century, and had a colourful and contentious history thereafter.[6]

THE CONTEMPORARY SIGNIFICANCE OF THE EPISTLES

The mark of modern study of the Epistles has been an awareness of their original setting and meaning; this does not mean that they have no contemporary significance but that that significance must be true to the original meaning. As we have noted, part of that awareness has been a rehabilitation of 2 and 3 John. Their apparently specific references offer the possibility of giving a clearer picture of the circumstances of the Johannine tradition which, in the Gospel and First Epistle, is notoriously difficult to place; in practice this has proved hard to achieve, although we have seen how a number of scholars have traced through them the later history of Johannine Christianity. More fruitfully, the tensions and conflict they imply offer a perspective from which Johannine thought and its potential can be evaluated. Since issues of authority, right belief and the boundaries of the community are at the centre of 2 and 3 John, the strengths and weaknesses of the distinctive Johannine approach to these can be explored.[7]

A more precise picture follows when 1 John is placed closely in relation to and subsequent to the Gospel; thus R. Brown discovers through the Epistles 'that the profound and innovative christology of GJohn also contained dangers, so that a

---

[6] Discussed by Brown, *Epistles*, 775–87; Westcott, *Epistles*, 193–9. There is some variety in the textual witnesses as to exact work order and placing.
[7] Lieu, *Second and Third Epistles*, 135–65.

drama of community history, religious sociology, and theological development unfolds before our eyes'.[8] For him, 1 John, at least in its original setting, was intended to present the definitive way of how the Gospel was to be read. Although we have rejected this as the original intention of 1 John, it is how it has been used in the history of exegesis and so begs the question whether 1 John should continue to act as a control on the interpretation of the Gospel – which is still as diverse in modern as in earlier times.[9] In this way a 'docetic' reading of the Gospel might be rejected on the grounds that it is excluded by the presence of 1 John in the canon; a number of scholars have remarked that E. Käsemann's presentation of Johannine theology in *The Testament of Jesus* sounds much like the supposed opponents of 1 John and have treated this as a basis for dismissing that presentation.[10] Yet this means 1 John chiefly serves to provide a framework for the Gospel rather than to be given heed in its own right.

The 'modern significance' of all this further emerges when this 'life-and-death struggle' within Johannine theology is seen as not so very different from the conflicts which plague the contemporary church.[11] However, while some of the issues may be the same, the social and ecclesiastical contexts are very different; we cannot move too lightly from one setting to the other in the hope of drawing far-reaching conclusions.

If we retain this awareness of the original circumstances of the letter as far as they can be deduced, four fundamental aspects of 1 John's response do remain central. The first is that the way and the terms in which faith is understood do matter;

---

[8] Brown, *Epistles*, x.

[9] Childs, *Canon*, 482–7, charges Brown with confusing the way 1 John functioned in the history of the canon with its original purpose, and, by interpreting it as intentionally polemical and tied to the Gospel, restricting the way it can be understood today. By contrast D. M. Smith, 'John, the Synoptics, and the Canonical approach to Exegesis', in *Tradition and Interpretation in the New Testament*, ed. G. F. Hawthorne and O. Betz (Michigan and Tübingen, 1987), 166–80 finds Brown's interpretation useful because it demonstrates the Gospel's susceptibility to being read in divergent and even contradictory ways and the need for a control or context such as that provided by 1 John and now by the canon.

[10] Brown, *Epistles*, 75; Burge, *Anointed Community*, 95, n. 197.

[11] Brown, *Epistles*, xv, presents this as the motivation for a commentary which introduces twentieth-century readers to this end-of-first-century struggle.

the development of doctrine as a defence against wrong belief as well as under the impulse of its own intellectual potential was and remains essential. New ideas and formulations need to be tested by their faithfulness to the faith as received from the past; sincerity alone does not guarantee that every expression of faith bears witness to the Jesus to whom the NT testifies. It may seem that 1 John errs on the side of cleaving to past tradition; it offers little encouragement to the equally important need to explore new formulations of faith in new contexts and little guidance as to how to do so. The Second Epistle appears to confirm that sense of a growing rigidity which could prove sterile, the repetition of formulae which no longer have a living, creative power. Yet in 1 John at least, the focus of what has been heard is very simple – the confession of Jesus together with mutal love; whether this is due to insight or to the limitations of the author's perspective, it may serve as a reminder that we do not need to consider everything from the past as equally important, or deserving preservation in the present regardless of ensuing conflict and schism. In the modern age this is not only true where conflict threatens the church but also in ecumenical dialogue – a situation which might seem foreign to 1 John and even inimical to 3 John if there we meet strained relations between churches with different traditions and different understandings of authority.

In fact the Johannine church has nothing to do with the modern denomination, reflecting as it does the many pressures peculiar to the nascent church against its Jewish background and in Graeco-Roman society. Yet what 1 John affirms in particular, even though without clear argument, is not timebound – that the forgiveness offered in Jesus rests on the reality of his humanity and death. This affirmation marked a crucial step in the development of the faith of the church when it was categorically maintained against tendencies which were more comfortable with Jesus' divinity than with his full participation in our common humanity, and it made clear that however his relationship with God is explored this is an aspect which cannot be compromised. The consequences of that affirmation for Christian living are only implicitly developed in 1 John and still need further development.

Secondly, the testing of statements of faith in the light of tradition and experience is the task and responsibility of the whole community of faith. This is because the letter does not see tradition as something objective which stands over against the believer and the community, but as an element within their total and corporate religious experience. Neither is there a particular office which holds an exclusive right to tradition and to its interpretation or evaluation. The experience of the whole community, grounded in what has been proclaimed and heard, stands in continuity with and is founded upon the first witness of those who physically saw and touched Jesus. In this way each generation of believers is dependent on the proclamation of the faith by those who have gone before, and most of all by the first witnesses to Jesus (1 John 1:1–4); at the same time the faith of each generation has its own integrity and is fully a sharing in eternal life.[12]

This leads naturally on to a third point, the central place 1 John gives to the confidence of the community. The expression of this confidence does have its negative side; there is little sense of the need to grow in faith and little visible commitment to the sharing of faith with those outside. Again 2 John may highlight the potential dangers of this, however much it was a natural response to the particular situation of the community. Yet, perhaps contrary to all appearances and perhaps in the face of their own crisis of confidence, 1 John affirms that believers are born of God, are children of God, do know God. This is not something that the community of believers can or do achieve themselves; it rests on what God has done and continues to do for them. That difficult but important dualist passage in 3:4–10 declares that the coming of Jesus has brought about the destruction of the power of evil and enables

---

12 This is emphasised by Childs, *Canon*, 486; 'the referent of the letter is the theological reality of the Gospel manifest in the human life of the believer', although in seeing this as excluding Brown's polemical/apologetic reading he pays too little attention to the original historical setting of the letter.

those who believe to live free of that power. This may sound like fantasy and invite the objection that nothing has changed, that 'all things have continued as they were from the beginning of creation' (2 Pet. 3:4). The response of 1 John is to appeal to the religious experience of believers and to point to the inner life of the community – thus offering a demand as well as assurance. The apparent exclusiveness of Johannine Christianity, which is less attractive to the modern reader than it was perhaps inevitable in its original setting, affirms that if Jesus' victory over sin is to be seen anywhere, it must be seen within the personal and even more the corporate life of those who believe.

For very different reasons a crisis of confidence of far greater proportions is often seen as a mark of this age, as is a consequent turning to different solutions for the individual; the church too may be affected by it and share the same hesitation and bewilderment. We may suspect that 1 John would not agree with the response to the back-slapping question, 'Are you a Christian?', 'I am *becoming* one.' Its celebration of Christian confidence cannot stand on its own, for it has its dangers, but its affirmation that the believer's relationship with God is assured because it rests in God must be upheld alongside the recognition that God's work has yet to be completed.[13]

With this we return, fourthly, to 1 John's insistence that in the life of the community belief and behaviour are inseparable from one another. It is not that behaviour is laid alongside experience as a further requirement so that the relative emphasis to be laid on each might be debated – as it has been at different stages in the church's history – but that the one does not truly exist unless it is manifested in the other. Thus 1 John sidesteps any suggestion that 'works' might put us right with God; behaviour is the test and the expression of a relationship with God which is initiated by God. This does not lead to moral passivity, waiting for God to do it; there is both exhortation and example. In practice 1 John does not give detailed ethical codes and has nothing to say about the moral dilemmas of living in the world.

[13] On this see Perkins, *Epistles*, 104–5.

Behaviour is focussed in the inner life of the community and the command to love one another. As we have just seen, if the victory of Christ over sin is to be seen anywhere, it must be within the common life of those who believe and who claim that victory. Thus this focus follows from 1 John's central concern for the community.

The letter also roots mutual love in the priority of God's action on behalf of those who believe, and of his character as light and as love. That 'God is love' (4:8, 16) has easily become disconnected from its context and placed as a central tenet in the Christian conception of God. This affirmation and the centrality given to mutual love naturally offer themselves as norms in the search for Christian standards of life and conduct: ' "God is love" is the central affirmation of biblical faith which forms the context in which all Scripture must be interpreted.'[14] Here caution is due; 1 John's concern is for the unity of the community of believers. The letter offers no guidelines as to how that love might be worked out in complex practical and ethical issues, and passes over in silence other norms of behaviour that the community may have observed. Yet love is not idealised or sentimentalised – love is not God; instead that God is love is only known in the sending of his Son for the sake of those he loved. Although not as clearly as in John, 'love is defined in terms of death' (3:16). 'The revelation of the Nature of God as love calls out a response in answer to that which is necessarily regarded as a "personal" call to men, and by suggesting the idea of unlimited self-communication as characteristic of God, it sets a type for human action. The nature of the believer must be conformed to the Nature of God.'[15]

Through all this we have seen something of a tension between the very specific original circumstances of 1 John and the potential of its language for a more universalising or conceptualising theological reflection. This is a potential

[14] R. Scroggs, *The New Testament and Homosexuality* (Philadelphia, 1983), 10, quoting the initiating sentence of the NT section in *Human Sexuality* (United Church of Christ, 1977), 57; this norm is then applied to that specific issue.

[15] E. C. Hoskyns and N. Davey, *Crucifixion–Resurrection* (London, 1983), 156–60 on the Fourth Gospel; the first quotation comes from p. 158; the second, from Westcott, *Epistles*, 149, on 1 John 4:16.

recognised at least since St Augustine's commentary and reflected in those studies which give 1 John a place within a systematic and thematic Johannine theology.[16] That tension is one that has its roots in the letter itself, born out of a polemical situation and yet far from restricted to polemics or apologetics. It is sharpened by the presence of 2 and 3 John, where historical context seem to outweigh theological insight. To see the letters' theology exclusively in terms of their historical response is to ignore the creativity of the author where he goes beyond his raw material of situation and tradition;[17] to speak only of the author's 'profoundly accurate and perennially normative formulation[s]'[18] is to ignore the particular historical inspiration and expression of those formulations, which may invite critical judgement. It is in the balance between the two that the Johannine Epistles' contribution to the theology of the New Testament is most distinctively heard.

[16] See above, p. 99, n. 2; we might add to them those which assume the intrinsic unity of their theological subject and so find a unity and depth of conception foreign to a more 'historical-critical' approach, such as Malatesta, *Interiority and Covenant*, whose uniting theme is that of religious experience. It is not accidental that such studies often find rich resources in the insights of past, 'pre-critical', particularly patristic, exegesis.

[17] Thus R. Schnackenburg, *Johannesbriefe* 33–4, rightly recognises that 1 John's 'mysticism' or language of immanence has yet to be given an adequate background in contemporary thought and concludes that the strongest element in Johannine theology is the religious personality of the author. See above, nn. 9, 12 on Child's criticism of Brown's polemical reading of 1 John on these grounds.

[18] Malatesta, *Interiority and covenant*, 2, speaking of the appeal to personal experience as the key to understanding the Epistle's literary form and theological meaning as a 'profoundly accurate and perennially normative formulation of what can be called Christian interiority, i.e. the conscious awareness of communion with the Father in and through Jesus Christ, and of the gifts that make possible and the obstacles that hinder such communion'.

Select bibliography

COMMENTARIES

J. L. Houlden's commentary marks a new stage in commentaries on
the Epistles, recognising as it does the importance of the polemical
situation of the letters for their interpretation and the need to explain
what the author was trying to do and the limitations of his approach.
R. Brown's commentary develops this most fully while also giving
detailed analysis of the background of the thought of the Epistle and
of different interpretations of its often opaque grammar and argument. His separation of detailed notes from more general comment
helps the reader avoid a sense of being swamped. K. Grayston alone
presents a sustained argument that 1 John precedes rather than
follows the Gospel, and his commentary includes many refreshing
insights, as does the short one of P. Perkins, which while not
uncritical is probably most accessible to the general reader. Schnackenburg's commentary is often cautious, but rewarding and perhaps
more sensitive to the theological insights of the letter than some of the
others. Of the older commentaries that by Brooke is based on the
Greek text and is the most thorough, often anticipating the conclusions of more recent study.

Brooke, A. E. *A Critical and Exegetical Commentary on the Johannine
    Epistles*, ICC, Edinburgh, 1912
Brown, R. E. *The Epistles of John*, AB30, New York, 1982
Bultmann, R. *The Johannine Epistles*, Philadelphia, 1973
Dodd, C. H. *The Johannine Epistles*, London, 1946
Gore, C. *The Epistles of John*, London, 1920
Grayston, K. *The Johannine Epistles*, NCB, Grand Rapids and
    Basingstoke, 1984
Houlden, J. L. *A Commentary on the Johannine Epistles*, London, 1973
Perkins, P. *The Johannine Epistles*, Dublin, 1980
Schnackenburg, R. *Die Johannesbriefe*, Freiburg, 1979

Smalley, S. *1, 2, 3 John*, World Biblical Commentary, Waco, 1984
Westcott, B. F. *The Epistles of St. John*, London, 1883

STUDIES

There are only a few specific studies of the Johannine Epistles. Those by Nauck and O'Neill propose specific theories about the origin and background of the Epistles, both of which raise some important points but have not proved convincing as a whole; Lieu uses a detailed analysis of 2 and 3 John to approach all three Epistles and the Johannine tradition generally. Brown's book is a readable presentation of his theory of the history of the Johannine community, finishing with the situation implied by the Epistles. The remaining books are collections of essays which include some discussion of the Epistles.

Brown, R. E. *The Community of the Beloved Disciple*, New York and London, 1979
Charlesworth, J. *John and Qumran*, London, 1972
Jonge, M. de *Jesus: Stranger from Heaven and Son of God*, Missoula, 1977
Lieu, J. M. *The Second and Third Epistles of John: History and Background*, Edinburgh, 1986
Nauck, W. *Die Tradition und der Charakter des ersten Johannesbriefes*, WUNT 3, Tübingen, 1957
O'Neill, J. C. *The Puzzle of 1 John*, London, 1966
Smith, D. M. *Johannine Christianity*, Edinburgh, 1987

THEOLOGY

Most of the studies which follow, except those of Bogart and Malatesta, are on 'Johannine' theology but give some independent place to the Epistles' contribution. As has been noted, this often leads to some degree of harmonising so that the Epistles are conformed to or read in the light of the Gospel.

Bogart, J. L. *Orthodox and Heretical Perfectionism in the Johannine Community as Evident in the First Epistle of John*, SBLDS 33, Missoula, 1977
Burge, G. *The Anointed Community. The Holy Spirit in the Johannine Tradition*, Michigan, 1987
Feuillet, A. *Le Mystère de l'amour divin dans la théologie johannique*, EBib., Paris, 1972
Forestell, J. T. *The Word of the Cross*, AnBib 57, Rome, 1974

Heise, J. *BLEIBEN. Menein in den johanneischen Schriften*, Tübingen, 1967

Lazure, N. *Les Valeurs morales de la théologie johannique*, Paris, 1965

Malatesta, E. *Interiority and Covenant*, AnBib 69, Rome, 1978

Okure, T. *The Johannine Approach to Mission*, WUNT 31, Tübingen, 1988

Vellanickal, M. *The Divine Sonship of Christians in the Johannine Writings*, AnBib 72, Rome, 1977

Index of references

Index of names

Index of subjects

This is not a comprehensive index, but is designed to be used along with the contents list and the index of references to help locate the main topics, chiefly of theological interest. Specific terms (such as 'propitiation' (*hilasmos*)) are best found in the index of references.

abide (*menein*) 29–31, 41–5, 94
author, 1, 4, 8, 12, 16, 23–7, 98
authority 12, 24–7, 91–2, 109

baptism 7–8, 30, 38, 45, 62, 66, 71, 77, 86
beginning (from the) 21, 30, 31, 32, 55, 71, 72, 82, 87, 105
belief 22–3, 44, 45, 52, 71–2, 75–8, 101–2, 112

Cain 35, 39, 53, 70, 87
Cerinthus 14–15, 76
command 32, 52, 55, 68, 94, 104
community 17, 25–6, 29, 31, 34, 39, 42–3, 47, 50, 53, 55, 62, 69–71, 78–9, 85–7, 88, 90, 93–4, 103, 106–7, 109, 117–19

dualism 35, 36–8, 40–1, 47, 55, 61–2, 65, 69–70, 80–7, 100, 108

Elder, the 8–9, 91–2
eschatology 28, 46–7, 55–6, 59, 61, 64, 73, 82, 88–90, 107, 109
ethics 44, 49–58, 106, 112–13, 118–19

gnosticism 14, 16, 20, 29, 33, 34, 38, 75, 80, 84
God: theocentricity 32, 41, 45, 66–7, 78–9, 103
God, children born of (*gennao, tekna theou*) 33–9, 40, 49, 78

of God (*ek theou*) 39–41
Gospel: relation with Epistles 6–7, 15–16, 16–21, 37, 47, 56, 63, 67–8, 70, 78, 85, 98–107, 114–15

Jesus 11, 14, 18–19, 23, 34, 45, 56, 63–4, 71–8, 86, 94–5, 101–3

know (*gignoskein*) 28, 32–3

life 22–3, 28, 55
love 53, 65–71, 106, 108, 119

Old Testament 20, 32, 37, 44, 63, 67, 80, 87
opponents 5, 8, 13–16, 22, 51, 60, 66, 70, 75, 77, 85, 88, 102, 113

Qumran 18, 20, 33, 37–8, 46, 57, 70, 82–3

sin 36, 52–3, 57, 58–65, 74, 77, 102–3, 108, 113
spirit 29–30, 34, 42–3, 45–9, 82–3, 105

tradition 8, 20, 24, 30–1, 45, 87, 94, 105–6, 110, 116–17

witness 12, 23–6, 48
world 39–40, 47, 54, 57, 69–70, 81, 83–5, 104